MW00439241

ENCOUNTER SERIES

Augustine Today

Essays by

William S. Babcock
Ernest L. Fortin
Robert J. O'Connell, S.J.
Eugene TeSelle

and
The Story of an Encounter by

John R. Muether

Edited and with a Foreword by
Richard John Neuhaus

WILLIAM B. EERDMANS PUBLISHING COMPANY
GRAND RAPIDS, MICHIGAN

Published by Wm. B. Eerdmans Publishing Co.
in cooperation with
The Rockford Institute Center on Religion and Society

Copyright © 1993 by Wm. B. Eerdmans Publishing Co.
255 Jefferson Ave. S.E., Grand Rapids, Mich. 49503

Printed in the United States of America

ISBN 0-8028-0216-8

Contents

Foreword

Of the holding of conferences there is no end, and I confess to having convened more than my fair share of them. But there really is no alternative. Not if we understand life in terms of a continuing conversation, from generation to generation. Tradition is making the past our own in the hope that the next generation will make that tradition — now, let us hope, not too badly distorted and maybe even slightly enhanced by our contribution — its own.

Of the many meetings issuing in this Encounter Series of books, I doubt if any more fully met my expectations as "Augustine Today." It was an intellectual and, yes, spiritual delight, and much of that delight comes through in John Muether's admirable "Story of an Encounter."

What is the connection between loving and knowing? Is the love of neighbor subordinated to the love of God, or do we love God through loving our neighbor? If we understand life in terms of *peregrinatio,* of pilgrimage toward God, can anything here on earth be taken with religious seriousness? Can thinking about body and soul, and especially about sexuality, ever escape the charge of being "dualistic"? Is community — whether the community of the church or the *polis* — ordered by truth, or is truth in service to the community? What are the alternatives, if there are any, to utopianism and *Realpolitik* in thinking about the civil order? Is there a "best regime" for the City of Man, or are all regimes under the judgment of the City of God? Or, for that matter, is the best regime the one that, paradoxically enough, knows that it is not the *very* best regime?

In all of Christian history, only Saint Paul has exercised a greater intellectual and spiritual sway than Saint Augustine. And even that must be qualified by the observation that much of what we take to be Pauline has been refracted through Augustine. The great achievement of Thomas Aquinas, it is said, was the synthesis of Aristotle and Augustine. It is preeminently Augustine who defines the Christian argument in that encounter. The same Augustine, however, is embraced by Martin Luther as an ally in rejecting the synthesis championed by Thomas and others. Does this mean that Augustine is a plastic figure who can be reformulated to any purpose? Hardly, as the papers and exchanges in this volume amply demonstrate. It is simply that wherever we go in the Christian intellectual tradition (at least in the West) we run into Augustine.

We discover that Augustine has been there before us. At least that is being discovered in this century, as Ernest Fortin points out in the conversation. Other construals of reality, especially those emerging from the Enlightenment, seem increasingly implausible, increasingly incapable of giving an adequate account of what we know and of what we know that we do not know. Perhaps Augustine's time is coming around again in a way that has not been the case for at least six hundred years. It is not only in theology, philosophy, and the history of ideas that Augustine is receiving a more careful hearing. Graham Walker, a participant in this conference, has recently written *The Moral Foundations of Constitutional Law* (Princeton University Press) in which he persuasively proposes explicitly Augustinian answers to some of the most pressing questions facing the right ordering of the *polis* today. Other examples of the rediscovered pertinence of Augustine could readily be multiplied.

Readers who have benefited from *Augustine Today* might want to pick up an earlier volume in this series, *Reinhold Niebuhr Today*. As the story of the conversation and the chapter by Eugene TeSelle in this volume make clear, the convergences and differences are instructive.

Many hands and minds make such conferences and books possible. I am, once again, most particularly indebted to Paul Stallsworth and Davida Goldman. And to Eerdmans Publishing Company for taking on the Encounter Series. The enthusiastic response to this project continues to be most gratifying.

Richard John Neuhaus
St. John the Evangelist
December 27, 1991
New York City

Cupiditas and *Caritas:* The Early Augustine on Love and Fulfillment

William S. Babcock

Augustine could put the question of human happiness with disarming simplicty. In the *De beata vita*, written at Cassiciacum in 386, within months of his conversion to catholic Christianity, he shows a startling, almost crude, directness in stating the issue. All persons want to be happy; and no persons are happy who do not have what they want (*De beata vita* 2.10). Augustine regarded these two points as truisms, acknowledged on all sides. No one — at least no one who understood the words — would disagree; and Augustine himself displays no doubt or hesitation about accepting them exactly as they stand. Nor is there any reason to suppose that he subsequently changed his mind. Decades later, in the *De trinitate*, he takes virtally the same tack: *Beatus igitur non est, nisi qui . . . habet omnia quae vult . . . (De trin.* 13.5.8). From the outset, then, Augustine regarded happiness as a matter of having what one wants; that is, so to speak, the fundamental structure of the question.

Another consideration, however, immediately comes into play. If it is true that no persons are happy who do not have what they want, it is not true, Augustine insists, that all persons who do have what they want are happy (*De beata vita* 2.10). Happiness is not simply a matter of having what one wants; it is also — and perhaps even more critically — a matter of wanting and having what will genuinely afford happiness to

1

human beings. Some things will not: a child may want to hold fire in his hands; but if he succeeds, he will not be happy. Having what he wants will bring only pain and wretchedness.

Most instances, of course, will be both more complex and less obvious than the relatively straightforward case of the child and fire. Consider a second, more complicated, example. Suppose that a person holds a position which brings wealth, pre-eminence, and power and which fulfills that person's long-cherished dream with regard to the standing that she would like to have in the world. At the same time, the position requires that she perform tasks and act in ways for which she is not suited by temperament, by character, or by abilities. In this case, holding the position that she wants, the person may believe herself happy and may actually feel happy (i.e., may actually take plea-sure at the way things stand in her life). Yet the fact that she must constantly act against the grain may well mean that, in truth, she is not happy at all, but is caught in a bitter tension, the strain of which she does not recognize and therefore does not acknowledge. If this description of the situation is plausible, then it will make sense to say that, despite her own belief and even despite her own feeling, the position is not actually one that does or can afford her happiness. It will also make sense to say that she is mistaken in her belief and in her feeling. Her happiness, we might say, is a mistake that she has made.

Suddenly, then, the issues connected with the question of happiness multiply. In the case of the child and fire, it is imme-diately obvious that a given object does not afford happiness. The child's cries of pain tell us so. In the more complicated case, however, there is no equivalent to the child's cries; and we are compelled to give up the simple correlation between what the person feels and what is actually true in that person's case. We are forced into a distinction between apparent happiness and genuine happiness; and, at the same time, we are forced to acknowledge that the ground for this distinction does not lie in the immediate beliefs and feelings of the persons in question (since those beliefs and feelings may be mistaken). It is in just this light, however, that the question of happiness becomes both important and urgent. What does make for happiness? What does not? How do we distinguish the one from the other?

How do we attain the one and avoid the other? Once we go beyond the straightforward case of the child and fire, these questions become immensely difficult. They require an account of what human beings are and of what will actually afford happiness to beings such as these. For genuine happiness will lie at the point of intersection of these two: what human beings are and what affords them happiness. And it will occur when human beings both want and attain what lies at the point of intersection (since there is no happiness that is not a having of what one wants).[1]

It would not be at all implausible, I think, to suppose that Augustine's entire philosophical-theological project, from beginning to end, was meant to supply answers to the questions we have just identified. Certainly Augustine himself believed that we have no other reason to take up philosophy — and his "philosophy" would include our "theology" — than to attain happiness: *Nulla est homini causa philosophandi, nisi ut beatus sit* (*De civ. Dei* 19.1). My aim in this study, however, is

---

1. The question of human happiness had had, of course, a long history in the intellectual and cultural traditions of antiquity before Augustine entered the discussion. For an account of many of the elements in that history, see Ragnar Holte, *Béatitude et sagesse. Saint Augustin et le problème de la fin de l'homme dans la philosophie ancienne* (Paris, 1962); and for a particularly fine elaboration of the way in which the problem took shape for and was addresed by Plato and Aristotle, see Martha C. Nussbaum, *The Fragility of Goodness: Luck and Ethics in Greek Tragedy and Philosophy* (Cambridge, 1986). Marcia L. Colish, *The Stoic Tradition from Antiquity to the Early Middle Ages*, 2 vols. (Leiden, 1985), chronicles the important Stoic contribution to the discussion on this matter (as on many others). I have tried, however, to devise a way of putting the question that would expose what was at issue and indicate what considerations were relevant without requiring a review of the antecedent discussion. Similarly, I have attempted to present Augustine's own views and arguments in a way that would show how they made sense — and what sense they made — in the light of his own approach to the question as he posed it, but I have not undertaken to identify their various affiliations with the Platonic, Christian-Platonic, and Stoic traditions on which he drew. While I hope that I have not misrepresented his thinking by failing to reckon with its antecedents, my aim has been to concentrate on Augustine himself rather than on his predecessors or on his use of those predecesors in reaching his own position.

not to attempt a characterization of Augustine's position on human happiness taken, somehow, as a whole and covering the entire span of his writings from the first dialogues of Cassiciacum to the final treatises against Julian of Eclanum and the monks of southern Gaul. I want rather to take on the more limited — although perhaps no less formidable — task of tracing certain developments in his thinking on this matter during the period between his conversion and the writing of the *Confessions,* the period which Eugene TeSelle has characterized as Augustine's apprenticeship in theology.[2] This period represents a tangled thicket of developments both in Augustine's life and in his thinking; and I do not want to pretend, even for a moment, that I am going to tackle them all. Too much was going on to permit any simple or simplified account. But it was during this period that Augustine gradually, and not without a certain amount of backing and filling, transposed the question of human happiness into the key of human love. My concern will be to discern the elements and to understand the outcome of that transposition.

I

Augustine's concern, of course, ran far beyond the individual cases of this person or of that. In distinguishing between what does and what does not genuinely afford human happiness and between what does and what does not count as true happiness,

2. See Eugene TeSelle, *Augustine the Theologian* (London, 1970), 59-182. The best single biographical treatment of this period in Augustine's life — as of his life as a whole — is still Peter Brown, *Augustine of Hippo: A Biography* (Berkeley and Los Angeles, 1967), 79-181. For the most part, in fact, I shall be concentrating on selected writings from the first few years following Augustine's conversion, for these strike me as the ones in which he effected the shift in his thinking about the question of happiness that I want to trace in this study. One key text comes, however, from *De diversis quaestionibus 83;* and it is difficult, if not impossible, to determine the dates of many of the individual articles that were compiled in this work (see the remarks of Oliver O'Donovan, "*Usus* and *Fruitio* in Augustine, *De Doctrinea Christiana I,*" *Journal of Theological Studies,* n.s. 33 [1982]: 374). The compilation took place around 395.

he was not thinking of particular instances but of what is true for human beings generally. Once again he could approach the matter with unnerving directness. In *De beata vita* (2.11) he asks what a person should obtain — since happiness is a matter of having what one wants — in order to be happy *(quid ergo sibi homo comparare debeet, ut beatus sit);* and the answer he proposes is that it should be something that can be had when it is wanted *(id, opinor, ei comparandum est, quod cum vult, habet).* Most things, however, are not available to us as wanted. Their comings and goings are not finally under our control and are, at best, only partially and impermanently amenable to our efforts. To look for happiness by obtaining the time-bound and fortuitous is, therefore, inevitably to put ourselves at risk of failure or loss, failure to obtain what we want or loss of what we want once we have obtained it. It is to make our happiness itself a fragile and treacherous thing: a matter of chance, attained at random, shattered by accident, perpetually under the threat of loss. It is to want a state of affairs that cannot possibly afford a secure and lasting happiness, for we cannot have such things as these when and for as long as we want *(quando volumus et quamdiu volumus).*[3]

Instead, Augustine argues *(De beata vita* 2.11), we must look to something quite different for our happiness, to something permanent and enduring *(semper manens)* that does not come and go according to the swings of fortune or the accidents of chance *(nec ex fortuna pendulum, nec ullis subiectum casibus).* Yet it might still seem otherwise. Twice in the *De beata vita* (2.11; see also 4.26-28) Augustine considers the instance of those fortunate persons — the pun *(fortuna, fortunati)* is certainly intended — who possess fortuitous things *(res fragiles casibusque subiectas)* in such abundance that they lack for nothing they want. By sheer wealth, it would seem, these people have se-

---

3. For Augustine, a happiness that is not secure and lasting will not count as genuine happiness. The very uncertainty about whether happiness will last — and the apprehensiveness this uncertainty breeds — undercuts the happiness. Later in his career, for just this reason, Augustine will make the certainty that their happiness will endure an essential ingredient in the bliss of the good angels; see, e.g., *De Gen. ad litt.* 11.17.22; *De civ. Dei* 11.11.

cured their happiness against happenstance; they have what
they want, when and as they want it, even though the things
they want and have are not *semper manentes*.

Still, no fortune, however vast, is secure against loss; and
it is impossible to love things that can be lost, Augustine insists,
without a sense of fear, i.e., precisely the fear of loss. In fact, the
more acute the person is, the more clearly the person will see
the risk and feel the apprehension (*De beata vita* 4.26). Consequently, since fear erodes happiness, no one who loves and
possesses such things can possibly be happy (*Non igitur haec
qui amat et possidet, potest ullo modo beatus esse*). Thus the wealthy
do not constitute a counterinstance. For genuine happiness, we
must look to what endures, to what no raging fortune can
snatch away (*nec ulla saeviente fortuna eripi potest*); and this,
Augustine proposes, is God who is *aeternus* and *semper manens*.
The person who is happy, therefore, is the person who has God.

The main lines of Augustine's argument are clear enough.
Since happiness comes from having what one wants — a statement that Augustine regards as true for all human beings — it
is clear that temporal things will not afford happiness: we
cannot have them in a way that corresponds to our wants. To
want such things, therefore, is to be like the child who wants
to hold fire in his hand. The upshot can only be pain and
wretchedness. The reason why this is so, however, is not that
temporal things bring immediate and obvious hurt. It is rather
that these things can, through time and circumstance, be lost
(or may never be attained) due to factors over which we do not
and cannot exercise full control. One's life may suddenly be
shattered by disease; one's lover may suddenly turn to another;
one's job may suddenly be terminated. The examples need not
be multiplied. The point is simply that, in relation to temporal
things and temporal states of affairs, we are always vulnerable
and there is no way finally to eliminate or to protect against
that vulnerability.

Vulnerability to loss, however, is not the same as loss
itself. One can still prosper in the temporal sphere while remaining vulnerable to loss; and in that prosperity, one can lose
(not one's vulnerability but) one's sense of vulnerability. That
is why the appropriate analogue to Augustine's view is not so

much the case of the child with fire as it is the instance of the woman whose position puts her under unacknowledged strain. Even though she has power and prestige, her position requires her to act against the grain and leaves her in tension. Even though people prosper in temporal matters, their prosperity can be lost; and, as a consequence, they are vulnerable still. The emotive mark of their vulnerabiity, Augusine insists, is fear *(metus)*.

II

Augustinian scholarship, so far as I can tell, has not paid much attention to the role of this notion of fear in Augustine's thought;[4] and, in particular, it has not noticed that it is precisely reference to this fear that seems to have prompted Augustine to shift — for the first and only time in *De beata vita* — from the vocabulary of wanting to the vocabulary of loving in his discussion of human happiness: fear is incompatible with happiness; and the person who loves things that can be lost cannot avoid fear.[5] Several years later, after his return to Africa from

---

4. A *Note complémentaire* — in *Bibliothèque augustinienne*, vol. 10: *Mélanges doctrinaux*, ed. G. Bardy, J. A. Beckaert, and J. Boutet (Paris, 1952), 716-17 — on Question 33 *(De Metu)* in *De div. quaest. 83* points to the Stoic origins of the notion and cites relevant passages from Nemesius of Emesa and Lactantius. It offers no comment, however, on the fact that, both in this text and in *De beata vita,* Augustine associates *metus* specifically with *amor* and, in doing so, alters the context (discussion of the "passions") in which the term and the concept appear in the Stoic tradition. It seems to me that, just as Augustine will later treat the "passions" as features of willing (see *De civ. Dei* 14.6; and, for brief discussion, my "Augustine on Sin and Moral Agency," *The Journal of Religious Ethics* 16 [1988]: 43-44), so he is in this early period treating them as functions of love — or rather, as we shall see, of a particular love. The discussion of fear and love in John Burnaby, *Amor Dei: A Study of the Religion of St. Augustine* (London, 1938), 214-16, has to do with fear in a quite different sense — fear of God or fear of (divine) punishment — for which, I suspect, Augustine more often uses the word *timor* than the word *metus*.

5. Holte, for example, summarizes the argument of this section of *De beata vita* without noting the quiet correlation of fear and love at all *(Béatitude et sagesse,* 196).

Rome, Augustine would make the relation between fear and love explicit: "It is beyond doubt that the one cause of fear is either that we will lose what we love after attaining it or that, despite all our hopes, we will never attain it at all" (*De div. quaest. 83* 33; my translation). Even before he left Cassiciacum, however, he was putting the link between fear and love to significant use in the *Soliloquia*, treating the fear of loss as a proof of love. The relevant passage is worth examining.

The *Soliloquia* record Augustine's intimate, internal dialogue with reason and, in the first book, probe the extent to which it is true that he desires to know, as he claims, only God and the soul, nothing more (*Sol.* 1.2.7). In this context, Augustine admits that, beyond his love for knowledge of himself and God, he may still love other things, for he finds that he can still be distressed at three points: by fear of losing (*metu amissionis*) those he loves, by fear (*metu*) of pain, and by fear (*metu*) of death. From this admission, reason then draws the following conclusion, converting Augustine's negative formulation into its positive counterpart: *Amas ergo et vitam tecum carissimorum tuorum, et bonam valetudinem tuam, et vitam tuam ipsam in hoc corpore: neque enim aliter amissionem horum metueres* (*Sol.* 1.9.16). The listing of Augustine's fears reveals the love that he suspects, but is not sure, he has: without the love, he would not fear the loss. Whatever may have been true with regard to the one instance in which fear and love are associated in *De beata vita*, the linking of the two has now become deliberate and by design.

"For you would not otherwise fear the loss of these." Reason's phrase has an accusing tone; and, in fact, the loves exposed by Augustine's fears turn out to be symptoms of a lingering but still potent disease of soul. In the same sequence of dialogue, reason goes on to ask whether Augustine would not, if he were suddenly to become convinced that both his body's health and his life with his cherished friends were secure and safe, be carried away with joy (*nonne . . . tibi etiam laetitia gestiendum est*). When Augustine agrees, reason drives the diagnosis home: *Omnibus igitur adhuc morbis amini et perturbationibus agitaris* (*Sol.* 1.9.16); and so long as Augustine is in this state, buffeted between fear and sudden joy, he has no reason to think that his soul is so purified that it can direct its gaze at God. The love associated with fear is plainly a misdirected love, a love gone wrong, that distracts from and competes with the single-minded pursuit of the divine. That is what makes it, in its emotive turbulence, a disease of soul. It seems clear enough, then, that the entire sequence of question and answer is designed to bring out a pathology of soul which has its roots in the love of things that can be lost and finds expression not only in fear of loss, but also in a kind of manic joy at the thought that such things might be safe.

Still more is to be learned from the *Soliloquia*. Near the end of the first book, pained at his lack of progress toward the divine, Augustine cries out that surely he has by now shown that he loves wisdom alone since "what is not loved in its own right *(propter se)* is not loved" and since it has now become clear, through reason's questioning, that he wants to have or fears to lose other things — life, tranquillity, friends — only for wisdom's sake (*Sol.* 1.13.22). In this last respect, he is referring back to the immediately preceding portion of dialogue in which reason had, once again, tested his attachment to various things other than wisdom itself. In this case, however, the result of reason's questions and Augustine's answers had shown that any lingering desire on Augustine's part for riches or his life with his friends or bodily well-being would arise only from his conviction that they might aid his pursuit of wisdom; and reason had concluded that it is not to be called desire *(cupiditas)* when things are sought *propter aliud,* for the sake of something else (*Sol.* 1.11.19; and generally *Sol.* 1.11.18–13.23).

This passage is important in several respects. First, it provides us with Augustine's earliest definition of love, even though the definition is, in this case, cast in negative form; what is not loved for its own sake and in its own right *(propter se)* is not actually loved at all (*Sol.* 1.13.22). Thus to love something will mean precisely to love it for itself, not as a means to something else for the sake of some other benefits that may accrue as a result of attaining it. Augustine will retain this definition, worded in one way or another, throughout the rest of his career. Second, it is important to notice that, given this definition, Augustine will have to discriminate between loves,

distinguishing one from another by referring to their objects,
i.e., by referring to *what* they love *propter se* and not *propter aliud*.
His definition is, in this regard, a formal definition: whenever
something is loved for its own sake, that counts as love. The
difference between loves, therefore, must lie in the things loved.
Finally, the passage indicates that Augustine has already settled
on a term for the love of things that can be lost, the love which
he associates with fear (and that association, we can now see,
is grounded in the objects loved: since they can be lost, love for
them will fear their loss). That term is *cupiditas;* for — once
again we have a negative formulation — when such things are
sought *propter aliud* (and thus, as the definition shows, are not
loved), the seeking of them is no longer to be called *cupiditas*
(*Sol* 1.11.19).

Just these points are confirmed by the account of love that
Augustine offers in the densely packed and difficult argument
that he presents in Questions 33-35 of the *De diversis quaestionibus 83*.[6] His point of departure is the declaration, which we
have already noted, that the only reason for fear *(metus)* is that
we might lose or might never attain what we love (*De div.
quaest. 83* 33). Fear, then, is a function of love;[7] and it is rooted,

---

6. Burnaby provides a nicely crafted summary of Augustine's argument (*Amor Dei*, 48). He does not note (except possibly by implication),
however, that the "analysis of the fear which makes happiness impossible"
with which Augustine begins is one that treats this fear specifically as a
function of a love (i.e., the love for things that can be lost); and, perhaps
for this reason, he does not fully bring out one crucial element in the
argument: the distinction that it draws between two loves. I might add,
however, that Burnaby is quite right, in my judgment, to treat *De div. quaest.*
33-36 as a unit. The more common practice seems to be to discuss Question
35 on its own (see, e.g., Holte, *Béatitude et sagesse*, 255-57; O'Donovan, "*Usus*
and *Fruitio*," 375). But the argument is unmistakably continuous from the
opening of Question 33 through the close of Question 35 and most probably through Question 36 (although, interestingly enough, Burnaby's own
summary does not take in Question 36).

7. Here, at the start of his argument, Augustine has not yet drawn
any distinction between loves. It will shortly become clear, however, that
he is using the association of fear and love to distinguish this love from
another, not marked by fear. Thus, more precisely stated, fear is not a
function of love *tout court*, but of love for things that can be lost — in short,
cupiditas.

Augustine suggests, in a complex emotive syndrome from which it cannot be separated and of which it is the chief symptom. The syndrome includes — in addition to fear itself — three other emotions, each of which is intimately linked to fear as its source or as its inevitable accompaniment: desire *(cupiditas)*, the love *(amor)* of transitory things, the loss of which we cannot help but fear; grief *(aegritudo* or *anxietudo)*, the psychic pain *(animi dolor)* we feel at the realization of our fears; and manic, baseless joy *(gestiens et vana laetitia)*, the rejoicing in things subject to loss which never quite cancels out the fear of loss *(De div. quaest. 83* 33).[8] Here we see, briefly and schematically laid out, the full pathology of soul that Augustine had begun to sketch in the *Soliloquia*. Its devastating effect upon the psyche is registered in the vividness of the verbs that he uses to describe the person who, lacking fear, lacks the syndrome's other emotions as well: *quem non exanimat metus, nec cupiditas eum vastat, nec aegritudo macerat, nec ventilat gestiens et vana laetitia (De div. quaest. 83* 33). Thus, if fear is a function of love, the love of which it is a function is specifically *cupiditas*, the

---

8. Note the echo here of the vocabulary that Augustine was already using in *Sol.* 1.9.16: *nonne . . . tibi etiam laetitia gestiendum.* To judge from Lactantius's report *(Inst.* 6.14.7), the (Latin) Stoics used a very similar vocabulary in their doctrine of the passions:

> Stoici affectus omnes, quorum impulsu animus commoveture ex homine tollunt, cupiditatem, laetitiam, metum, maestitiam [i.e., *aegritudo,* see below], quorum duo priora ex bonis sunt aut futuris aut praessentibus, posteriora ex malis. Eodem modo haec quattuor morbos, ut dixi, vocant non tam natura insitos quam prava opinione susceptos et idcirco eos censent exstirpari posse radicitus, si bonorum malorumque opino falsa tollatur. Si enim nihil censeat sapiens bonum, nihil malum, nec cupiditate ardescet, nec laetitia gestiet, nec metu tenebitur, nec aegritudine contrahetur.

Augustine — whether this is the source of his vocabulary or not — has significantly altered the Stoic pattern by (a) treating *cupiditas* as *amor rerum transeuntium* and thus making it the root of the other three passions and (b) showing that, once *cupiditas* is uderstood in this sense, fear is not only a passion in its own right, but also an inescapable aspect of all the others. In effect, he has made the traditional doctrine of the passions over into a depiction of the psychic effects of love for things that can be lost. His pathology of soul is the pathology of this love.

love of transitory things; and the consequence of that love is not only fear as a distinct emotion in its own right but an emotional life tinged with apprehensiveness at every point.

Now we could eliminate fear at a stroke, Augustine argues, if we were to make fearlessness itself the object of our love.[9] By itself, however, fearlessness is hardly the answer. It is most certainly characteristic of a cadaver or of an audacity completely blind to risk (*De div. quaest. 83* 34). What we should love, therefore, is not fearlessness alone, but rather fearlessness coupled with life (as opposed to the cadaver) and with understanding (as opposed to the *audax*).[10] But what of our love itself? Is that also, along with life and understanding, something that we should love in addition to fearlessness (*De div. quaest. 83* 35.1)?

Even in its original context, the question seems artificial and more than a little strained.[11] It is significant, however, because it prompts Augustine to draw explicitly — although rather clumsily — a distinction that is critically important in his understanding of love (and that was, we have suggested, already tacitly at work in the *Soliloquia*). He now makes it quite plain that we are to distinguish between loves and that the distinction is to be made precisely with reference to their objects (*De div. quaest. 83* 35.1). Augustine first answers his question by insisting that we should, of course, love our love: without it, we would not love life and understanding. But he immediately enters qualifications.

First, to love something is to desire *(appetere)* it for its own sake and in its own right *(propter se)*; and how can we say that

---

9. Augustine's argument on this score is obscure (see *De div. quaest. 83* 33 *ad init.*) and is chiefly designed, I suspect, to bring him to his next point. It is not necessary to repeat or to assess it here.

10. *De div. quaest. 83* 35.1. O'Donovan is misled, I think, when he says that *De div. quaest. 83* 35 "starts from an *a priori* premise that the object of love is 'intelligent life without fear'" ("*Usus* and *Fruitio*," 375). The "premise" is, in fact, the conclusion Augustine draws from the preceding argument of Questions 33 and 34.

11. I think it would be fair to say, however, that in its context the question (should we love our love?) is roughly equivalent to asking whether we should approve or endorse our love.

love is to be desired for itself alone when, in the absence of its object *(quando desit quod amatur)*, love is obviously wretched *(indubitata miseria)*? Thus love must be assessed with reference to its object (rather than simply with reference to itself) and, specifically, with reference to the presence or absence of its object. Furthermore, love is a kind of motion *(motus quidam)*; and motion is always toward some object. Consequently, when we ask what we ought to love, we are asking what it is toward which it is right for us to be moved *(quid sit illud ad quod moveri oporteat)*. On these grounds also it is clear that love is to be assessed in relation to its object. For there is also, Augustine adds, a shameful *(turpis)* love in which the soul pursues things inferior to itself; and this love is better called *cupiditas*, "the root of all evils" (1 Tim. 6:10).

In the subsequent development of his argument, Augustine goes on to show, as we might expect, that the antithesis of *cupiditas* is love of the eternal — of which alone we can rightly be confident that it cannot be snatched away from its lover — and to equate the eternal, once again, with God (*De div. quaest. 83* 35.2). This love, as love of what should be loved, he labels *caritas* or *dilectio* (*De div. quaest. 83* 35.2); and just as he associates *cupiditas* with 1 Timothy 6:10, he associates *caritas* with Matthew 22:37 (the command to love God with all one's heart, soul, and mind) and with John 17:3 (the assurance that eternal life consists in knowing the one true God and Jesus Christ as sent by God). But we do not need to follow out the details of the argument in order to see how Augustine achieved his discrimination between loves — and I would want to insist that he was not distinguishing *cupiditas* from love but was distinguishing *cupiditas* and *caritas* precisely as two loves.[12]

---

12. I do not, of course, mean to imply that, either before or after writing *De div. quaest. 83* 35, Augustine sorted out and consistently used his vocabulary according to this scheme — keeping *amor/amare* as the general terms and reserving *cupiditas/cupere* and *caritas/dilectio/diligere* for love of transitory and love of eternal things respectively. There is no "lexicographical" answer to the question of Augustine's view of love (see O'Donovan's apt remarks in *The Problem of Self-Love in St. Augustine* [New Haven and London, 1980], 10-11). I would want to maintain, however, that once he had worked out this distinction between two loves — which, for

It is important, however, to be careful in stating the point. I do not think that, in this regard, we can speak of two different kinds or forms or aspects of love, as if they arose from different locations within the soul or involved different approaches on the part of the lover toward what is loved.[13] Augustine is working — here as in the *Soliloquia* — with a single definition of love; and he does not alter or add to it in order to accommodate either *cupiditas* or *caritas*. Each is a case of desiring something for its own sake; and, therefore, each is a case of love. Augustine does not distinguish between them by varying his ideas of love. Rather he discriminates between the two by referring to the object that each pursues, the transitory or the enduring, the temporal or the eternal, what can be lost or what cannot. The emotive differences between the two loves do not precede but rather reflect and follow from their distinctive objects. In speaking of love for the eternal (*De div. quaest. 83* 35.2), Augustine remarks that what is loved necessarily affects its lover with something of itself *(quoniam id quod amatur, afficiat ex se amantem necesse est)*. His immediate point is that the eternal, as the object of love, will tincture the soul with eternity. But in its more general form, the remark holds good for the transitory as well. It too, when loved, will tincture the soul with something of itself — in his case, the vulnerability of loss that shows itself in fear and in the entire pathology of soul that Augustine links with his analysis of fear. It is in loving what does not genuinely afford human happiness that we make ourselves unhappy.

It is important, however, to recognize that Augustine's account of human unhappiness goes well beyond the emotive

---

the sake of convenience, I will continue to label *cupiditas* and *caritas* — he retained the distinction throughout his career (although it should also be noted that gradually, from about 395 on [see *De doct. chr.* 1.22.21], he replaced *cupiditas* with a notion of *amor sui* as the antithesis of *caritas*).

13. I follow O'Donovan in his argument that it is not appropriate to speak of different kinds of love, immanently distinguished (i.e., in the loving subject), in Augustine's view. On the other hand, the various "aspects of love" that O'Donovan does differentiate do not seem to me to have come into play as yet at this early stage in the development of Augustine's understanding of love. See the discussion in O'Donovan, *Problem of Self-Love*, 10-36.

unease of the person who looks for happiness where it cannot be found. *Cupiditas* is not only a love that afflicts the lover with apprehensiveness; it is also the "root of all evils" (1 Tim. 6:10). Certain features of Augustine's analysis of evil, and specifically of human moral evil, in the *De libero arbitrio* will show how this is so. No blame attaches, Augustine insists, to the desire *(cupiditas)* to live without fear (*De lib. arb.* 1.4.9).[14] Life without fear is, in fact, a great good and is desired by all, both the good and the evil. But the good seek it by turning their love *(amor)* away from things that cannot be had without the risk of loss, while the evil, eager to enjoy these things with security, try to remove all impediments to their enjoyment and thus fall into the most vicious crimes, leading a life that might better be called death (*De lib. arb.* 1.4.10). The crimes in question are, of course, crimes against other persons, for they are the ones who might impede or endanger secure enjoyment of what can be lost. And it is *cupiditas,* the *amor* for things that can be lost against one's will (*De lib. arb.* 1.4.10), that gives birth to this desperate sense that others constitute a threat to self. Fearing loss, it seeks to secure against loss by removing or by dominating others so as to eliminate the threat they represent. In this sense, it sets one person against another. The only answer to it is another love, or rather love for another object that is not vulnerable to loss, for that alone will remove the fear of loss.

Furthermore, *cupiditas* represents, in Augustine's view, a demeaning of the self, a violation of its value. For Augustine, human beings are constituted in a pattern that instantiates an ordered hierarchy of values. At the peak of this hierarchy stands the mind or reason, which human beings do not share with other living things that are merely animate or sensate but do not have the capacity to reason. What distinguishes human beings from the beasts (and enables them to tame the beasts even though the beasts are greatly superior in sheer physical strength) is also, then, what holds the highest value in the

---

14. In *De lib. arb.* 1, Augustine's vocabulary includes a distinction between culpable and nonculpable *cupiditas* (see, e.g., *De lib. arb.* 1.3.8–4.10). Therefore, he can use the term for blameless as well as blameworthy desire (the former he might, in other contexts, have designated *appetitus*).

internal constitution of human beings themselves.[15] *Cupiditas*
violates the value of mind or reason in two senses. On the one
hand, it subjects the mind to the emotive syndrome that we
have already identified, tangling it in the wild swings of emotion that go with fear and empty joy, and preventing it from
clearly distinguishing truth and falsehood.

> . . . the soul is dominated by lust [*libido*, a synonym for *cupiditas*
> in the vocabulary of the *De lib. arb.*; see *De lib. arb.* 1.3.8–4.9] . . .
> now approving falsehood as if it were truth . . . now holding its
> assent back, and often fearing the most obvious reasonings, now
> despairing of ever finding the truth and sticking in the dark pit
> of folly, now attempting to reach the light of intelligence, and
> again falling back in sheer weariness. Meanwhile, the cupidities
> (*cupiditatum*) exercise their dominion tyranically and disturb the
> man's whole mind and life with varying and contrary tempests,
> fear (*timor*) on one side, longing (*desiderium*) on the other; here
> anxiety (*anxietate*), there vain and false rejoicing (*inani falsaque
> laetitia*); here torture because something loved has been lost
> (*cruciatu rei amissae quae diligebatur*), there eagerness to obtain
> what it does not possess (*ardore adipiscendae quae non habebatur*).
> . . . (*De lib. arb.* 1.11.22)[16]

It is important to observe, however, that Augustine is *not* opposing emotion to reason *tout court* here. Rather he is describing
the adverse effects of a certain emotive pattern, the pattern
derived from and associated with *cupiditas*, on reason. There is
also, as we shall see, an emotive pattern that coheres with and
enhances reason's value.

Cupiditas also demeans the self by bringing the mind into
subjection to things over which it ought properly to rule. With
regard to the things that can be lost against one's will,

---

15. For Augustine's argument in support of the view that human
beings are constituted in a hierarchical order with mind or reason at its
peak, see *De lib. arb.* 1.7.16–9.19.

16. The translation is from John H. S. Burleigh, ed., *Augustine: Earlier
Writings* (Philadelphia, 1953), 125-26. Augustine regards the condition he
describes here as penal; but it is a penalty internal to — rather than exter-
nally imposed on — *cupiditas* and therefore can rightly be considered an
account of the emotive character and consequence of *cupiditas* as love of
transitory things.

Augustine observes that some persons use them well, others badly. The latter are those who cling to them in love and become interwoven wth them, who make them virtually members of their souls *(velut membra sui animi)* so that, when these things begin to be cut off, they are cruelly disfigured and go into decline *(De lib. arb.* 1.15.33). In this way, they subordinate themselves to things that ought to be subordinate to them. The fault, of course, does not lie with the things. They are good and are no more to be blamed than gold is to be blamed for avarice, or food for gluttony, or wine for drunkenness. Rather, the fault lies in the bad use that occurs when people turn away from things that are divine and genuinely enduring *(divinis vereque manentibus)* and pursue things that are uncertain and changeable *(mutabilia atque incerta)*. This in turn amounts to a reversal of values both in the world and in the self, taking the lower for the higher and demeaning the mind to the level of what it loves *(De lib. arb.* 1.15.33–16.35). In this one genus, Augustine suggests, all evil acts *(malefacta)*, all sins *(peccata)*, are contained *(De lib. arb.* 1.16.34-35). What is at stake in the question of human happiness, therefore, is a great deal more than the apparently naive having of what one wants. Also at issue are the morality of relations between persons and the realization of the value of the self.

III

What should a person obtain in order to be happy? In *De beata vita,* as we have seen, Augustine answered that it should be something that can be had as wanted; and this is the permanent and enduring, the eternal, which is God. Thus the person who is happy is the person who has God *(De beata vita* 2.11: *Deum igitur . . . qui habet, beautus est).*

In *De beata vita,* Augustine did not connect either the wanting or the having of God in ways that would be significant for the subsequent development of his thinking on this score. Several points are to be noted. First, having God could and did mean living a certain kind of life and attaining a certain character. The person who has God, it would seem, is the person

who lives uprightly *(bene)* and who attends to God and keeps
to God alone *(qui Deum attendit et ad ipsum solum se tenet)*. Yet
difficulties immediately emerge. This delineation of the person
who "has" God, it turns out, is less than fully satisfactory, for
it actually describes one who seeks God, and one who seeks
does not yet have *(qui autem Deum quaerit, nondum habet Deum)*.
The problem is clear enough and might be stated in the form
of a dilemma: either we can say that the person who seeks God
is happy and give up the notion that happiness entails having
what one wants, or we can maintain that happiness does come
from having what one wants and admit that the person who
seeks God is not only not happy, but is wretched — since, as
Augustine insists throughout *De beata vita*, the person who is
not happy is wretched *(miser)*.[17]

On this point, it seems to me, the discussion in *De beata
vita* remains inconclusive — despite the fact that it shows considerable ingenuity in looking for ways to make one horn or
the other of the dilemma palatable, or even to avoid the
dilemma altogether. It is clear, however, that Augustine does
not surrender or modify his claim that happiness involves
having what one wants; and this fact suggests, already at this
earliest stage in his thinking on the matter, that he will need to
find another idiom in which to conceive and to discuss the
having of God. He will need — as it will turn out — to speak
of having virtue by living virtuously and, in this sense, keep a
tenuous grip on the notion of happiness as having what one
wants; but having virtue is not the same as having the eternal
or having God. These one has by knowing them.[18]

---

17. For the discussion that I have summarized here, see *De beata vita*
2.12–3.22 (the Latin phrases cited in the text come respectively from 3.18
and 3.19). For the claim that everyone who is not happy — i.e., does not
have what he or she wants — is wretched, see 2.11.

18. Here again, we have a case in which — once Augustine has
brought all the factors into place — love is determined by its object.
Without making an excursion into his metaphysics and his philosophy of
mind, we can at least say that, for Augustine, the eternal (God) belongs to
the realm of the intelligible rather than the sensible, the incorporeal rather
than corporeal, the invisible rather than the visible. Therefore, the eternal
will be available and accessible to human beings only through the mind

The process of replacement began even before Augustine left Cassiciacum. It is evident in the *Soliloquia;* and perhaps it is no accident that the *Soliloquia* is also the work in which the theme of love first takes a significant place in Augustine's discussion of what does (as opposed to what does not) genuinely make for human happiness.[19] As we have noted, Augustine's aim in this work is to attain knowledge of God and of the soul. Such knowledge, however, requires a cleansing of the knower, a purging of both false conceptions and moral impurities. Love enters Augustine's discussion of this purification process in two ways.

Conceiving the soul's approach to God under the imagery of the eyes and seeing, Augustine says that three things are required: that the soul have sound eyes with which to see, that it direct its gaze to God, and that it actually see. For the first two of these — the healing of the eyes and the directing of the gaze — the soul must have faith, hope, and love (the reference to 1 Cor. 13:13 is obvious): faith *(fides)* that it can see only if it is healthy and that the thing to which it directs its gaze will, when seen, make it happy; hope *(spes)* that it can, in fact, be cured and that if it does rightly direct its gaze, it will see; love *(caritas)* for the promised light and as the desire to see and to enjoy *(qua videre perfruique desideret)* the object of its gaze. In the

---

and its capacities for thought and reason. These represent the sole avenue of human approach to and possession of the intelligible. Thus, if love is to attain this object at all, it must attain it through the mind and the mind's knowing of it. It might be worth adding that, even in those cases in which Augustine entertained the notion that the possession of virtue might constitute happiness, he looked for some way to link virtue to the eternal (see, e.g., *De beata vita* 4.33-36 and *De lib. arb.* 1.13.28–15.31).

19. O'Donovan observes that *De moribus ecclesiae catholicae* "marks Augustine's determination to convert the Christianized Neoplatonism of the Cassiciacum dialogues into theology, and to speak in terms of the love of God, as the Bible does. It is from this point that the verb 'to love' begins to dominate his teleological thought, an innovation on the classical tradition that has not been accorded sufficient notice" (*"Usus* and *Fruitio,"* 375). It seems to me that this process was already under way in the *Soliloquia* (although I am not sure that I would want to suggest that Augustine ever came to a position that was not, in some form, a Christianized Neoplatonism).

final stage — seeing — neither faith nor hope will still be necessary. Love, however, will not only remain, it will be increased. In fact, the soul will be able to continue in that happiest of visions (*beatissima visione*) only insofar as love keeps its eyes fixed upon God. In one sense, then, love is sustained by faith and hope, the belief that one can, and the hope that one will, achieve sight. In another, however, love underlies both faith and hope (if there were no love, who would care about seeing or bother to hope that it might be achieved?); and, in the end, it becomes the emotive mode in which the cognitive vision is realized: if there were no love, the sight would not hold the self enthralled. And Augustine's vocabulary hints — since hope's hope is to see and to enjoy God — that he will construe love in this sense (i.e., when it has attained what it desired) as the enjoyment of its object (*Sol.* 1.6.12–7.14).[20]

Immediately following the development of this theme the *Soliloquia* turns to reason's interrogation of Augustine concerning the exclusiveness of his love for knowledge of God and the soul. In this context (*Sol.* 1.9.16; 11.19), as we have already seen, reason uses the listing of Augustine's fears to expose his loves (in the sense of *cupiditas*) and then turns this conclusion on its head by showing that they no longer count as loves since Augustine seeks them only for the sake of something else (*propter aliud*). Now, however, we can see what is at stake in the interrogation. The aim is to discover what sort of lover of wisdom Augustine is (*qualis sis amator sapientiae*); and, in vivid imagery, reason shows why the question is important (*Sol.* 1.13.22). Suppose that you were aflame with love for a beautiful woman. Would she not be quite right to keep herself from you, if she were to discover that you loved anything other than her (*praeter se*)? And will the pure beauty of wisdom show itself to you, if you do not burn for it alone? It is this image that evokes from Augustine the cry that surely he has shown that he loves

---

20. For a more extensive discussion of this passage — although concentrating on hope rather than love — see Basil Studer's essay, "Augustine and the Pauline Theme of Hope," in *Paul and the Legacies of Paul*, ed. William S. Babcock (Dallas, 1990).

nothing else, since what is not loved for its own sake and in its own right *(propter se)* is not loved at all *(Sol.* 1.13.22). Thus the tacit definition of love — only love of something for its own sake counts as love — reinforces the claim that love for wisdom, love for God, must be exclusive. It does not permit love for anything else. Thus, in the *Soliloquia,* Augustine has not only intertwined loving God and knowing God in a way that foreshadows — as we shall see — his answer to the question of how we come to have the eternal, i.e., how we attain happiness; he has also made it clear that this love must be love for God alone.

In the *Soliloquia,* however, the question of human happiness — as Augustine had framed it in *De beata vita* — remains largely implicit rather than explicit in the text. It is clearly present as a major element in Augustine's thinking; but it comes to the surface only here and there in the occasional choice of words or turn of phrase. The full — although not necessarily final — integration of the newly intertwined themes of loving and knowing with the question of the attainment of happiness occurs rather in the rich and complex argument of *De moribus ecclesiae catholicae,* written in 388. In this work, too, Augustine first makes it fully clear just how we are to construe the attainment of happiness as the realization of the human good. He starts, once again, with the universally human desire to live happily. But he now states the problem, from the outset, in terms of having (not what one wants but) what one loves. Those who do not have what they love or who have what they love if it is hurtful *(noxium)* or who do not love what they have even though it is the best *(optimum)* are not happy *(De or.* 1.3.4). Happiness resides rather in a fourth alternative: when that which is the human best *(hominis optimum)* is both loved and had *(et amatur et habetur).* For, Augustine asks, what else does enjoyment *(frui)* mean but to have present what one loves *(nisi praesto habere quod diligis)*? Thus happiness comes with the enjoyment of the human best. If we plan *(cogitamus)* to live happily, our best must be present to us *(De mor.* 1.3.4).

What, then, are we to understand as the *optimum hominis?* The answer to that question will depend, at least in part, on what human beings are (just as what is best for the woman in our opening example will depend, at least in part, on what her temperament, character, and abilities are). On this point, we must reduce Augustine's argument to the barest summary. Nevertheless, it is important at least to indicate the view he held and how he held it.

Augustine construes human beings as so composed of body and soul that the body is at its best when it is appropriately cared for and properly governed by the soul (*De mor.* 1.4.6–5.8). Consequently, he regards the human *optimum* as that which will bring the soul to its best (so that it will, among other things, exercise the right care for and governance of the body). What perfects the soul is virtue. But virtue, although a disposition or quality of the soul, is only attained by seeking something other than and beyond the self; and it comes as no surprise that Augustine should insist that this "something," which raises the human to its best, must not be subject to loss (*De mor.* 1.6.9-10). His argument is by now familiar: it is impossible to have confidence in a good that can, one senses, be snatched away, against one's will, even though one wants to hold and to embrace it (*De mor.* 1.3.5). Thus, given the sort of beings that human beings are, the "something" that will bring them to their best can be nothing less than God. With this conclusion, set in this context, Augustine discovers that he has a formula that will allow him to distinguish between seeking and having without reducing the seeker to the level of mere wretchedness: if we pursue (*sequimur*) God, we live rightly (*bene*); if we attain to (*assequimur*) God, we live not only rightly, but happily (*De mor.* 1.6.10). Living rightly is not the same as having God and therefore cannot be construed as happiness; but it is the way in which we live out our longing for the God in whom we will attain happiness.[21]

Here we come upon what is perhaps the great achieve-

---

21. This formula is not, of course, a solution to the dilemma that emerged in *De beata vita* (see above, p. 18). But it does represent a tacit acknowledgment (anticipated, perhaps, in *De beata vita* [4.35] itself) that not all forms of "not being happy" are on the same footing. Living rightly is not yet happiness; but it is certainly not to be reckoned in the same category with the unhappiness of loving what can be lost. It belongs to another love, a love that will be happy when it does attain its object.

ment of *De moribus ecclesiae catholicae:* the integration of the virtuous life into the life of love. It is important to note the setting in which this integration occurs. How, Augustine asks (*De mor.* 1.7.10), are we to pursue God whom we do not see? And how are we to see? God is seen, not with the eyes, but with the mind; and in our present condition, our minds are enveloped in a dark cloud of folly, unfit and unable to see. In this condition, Augustine maintains, we must rely on the teachings of authority rather than our own darkened reason for direction in our pursuit of God (*De mor.* 1.7.10; cf. 1.2.3); and authority's direction comes, in particular, in Christ's command that we are to love God with all our heart, all our soul, and all our mind (*De mor.* 1.8.13). The ultimate good that Christ prescribes for us is, no doubt, that which he commands us to strive after with our best and deepest love *(summo amore)*. From his command, then, we learn both what we are to love and how much we are to love it (*De mor.* 1.8.13), that God is our highest good *(nobis summum bonum)*, and that we must refer all our purposes to this one thing *(ad id omnia consilia nostra referenda)*. It is clear, therefore, that Augustine makes his appeal to the love-command specifically in relation to a cognitive problem, the problem of coming to see God with the mind, which he describes in obvious continuity with his previous discussion of knowing and loving in the *Soliloquia*. The love into which Augustine will integrate virtue in *De moribus ecclesiae catholicae* is the love that he has already intertwined with knowing in the earlier work.

Augustine's interpretation of virtue as the various dispositions of love itself *(ipsius amoris vario quodam affectu)* is well known and need not be rehearsed again here in great detail. Augustine defines virtue as our best and deepest love of God *(summam amorem Dei)*; and he construes the four classical virtues — *temperantia, fortitudo, iustitia,* and *prudentia* — as characteristics of this love (*De mor.* 1.15.25; 19.35–25.47). Perhaps the most important thing for our purposes is simply to note that Augustine here clearly and explicitly identifies a person's love as that which forms the person's character — and that, as we would expect, he discriminates between loves by discriminating between the objects loved. Commenting on Paul's exhortation that we "be not conformed to this world" (Rom. 12:2), he makes the double point: persons are conformed to what they love (De mor. 1.21.39: *ei rei quemque conformari quam diligit*). Thus it is not love that forms the self in virtue, but specifically love for God.

This view, however, creates a strange echo of the virtues in other loves.[22] Temperance, for instance, is love keeping itself whole and incorrupt for God; but other loves will also have a temperance of their own insofar as they give themselves entirely to what they love. Similarly fortitude is love enduring all adversity for the sake of God. Yet other loves will also endure great hardships for the sake of their objects; and Augustine can urge that lovers of God ought to be ready to endure a good deal more in their striving for God than lovers of gold or women do in their indefatigable efforts to attain what they love (De mor. 1.22.41). Thus, the virtues, in Augustine's treatment of them, cease to be good in their own right; they are good only insofar as the love of which they are the dispositional expressions is itself good — which is to say, insofar as it is love of God. In intergrating virtue in love's striving for its object, then, Augustine has eliminated the possibility that the virtues might be understood as the attainment of happiness. Virtue, living rightly, finds its context in love's striving for God; and happiness belongs rather to love's attainment of God.

Within the context to which they properly belong, the virtues do, of course, play a crucial role in Augustine's view. They are the dispositional qualities through which persons ward off or overcome the pulls and tugs of their other loves. The function of temperance (De mor. 1.19.35) is to control and quiet the *cupiditas* that, in drawing us away from God and from the enjoyment of the divine goodness, is "the root of all evil" (1 Tim. 6:10). It reverses the enslavement of the self to those things that should properly be subject to it by reducing their status, so to speak, from objects of love to objects of use.[23] The

---

22. It is noteworthy that, in De mor. 1.15.25, Augustine actually offers a double definition of the virtues, once as the dispositions of love and then as the dispositions, specifically, of love for God.

23. O'Donovan is wholly right, it seems to me, in his double claim

vir temperans will not love mortal and transitory things *(rebus mortalibus et fluentibus)*, will desire none of them in its own right *(per se appetendum)*, but will treat them *utentis modestia, non amantis affectu (De mor.* 1.21.39). For, as we have seen, it is precisely the use of things for some further purpose that proves we do not love them for themselves. Similarly, fortitude overcomes the fear of loss that marks the love of temporal things and, in particular, the fear *(terror)* of bodily pain or, above all, death. Thus love of God shows temperance in not desiring mortal things and fortitude in losing them *(De mor.* 1.22.40: *in non appetendis istis temperans, in amittendis fortis)*.

The same pattern governs Augustine's brief discussions of justice and prudence. Justice gives to each its own by serving only God and, with regard to everything else, ruling the things already subjected to the self and presuming that the rest are to be brought into the same subjection *(De mor.* 1.24.44). Prudence, finally, guards against deceit, keeping the soul vigilant against the daze in which, in little acts of self-deception, it allows itself to be pulled off course *(De mor.* 1.24.25). The virtues function, then, as the collective antidote to *cupiditas* and to the emotive syndrome Augustine associates with it. They undo the demeaning of the self that occurs when *cupiditas* draws it down into subjection to the things it ought to rule. They do so, however, only as the dispositions of a love that is striving for God; and they do not yet represent either the full realization of the value of the self or the attainment of happiness, the having of God.

For these we must return to the idiom of knowing with which Augustine frames his discussion of the virtues. Augustine himself points us in this direction. At the end of his discussion of the virtues in *De moribus*, he dwells momentarily on eternal life as the great prize of love's striving after God *(De mor.* 1.25.47). But eternal life — Augustine cites John 17:3

that "just as *fruitio* presents itself in Augustine's earliest writing independently of *usus*, so *usus* is independent of *fruitio*" and that, in this early usage, " 'use' is quite clearly opposed to 'love' " *("Usus* and *Fruitio,"* 376). It seems clear, then, that Augustine had established the pairing of *usus* and *amor* before he came to the pairing of *usus* and *fruitio*. Thus it was only natural that, when he did pair *usus* and *fruitio*, *fruitio* and *amor* would converge.

directly — is to know the one true God and Jesus Christ whom God has sent. Thus the culmination of love's striving, the attainment of its object, comes not in virtue but in knowledge, the knowledge that virtue makes possible by its cleansing of the mind from its misconceptions and moral misdirection, from its entanglement in the emotive syndrome of *cupiditas*. It is in *De diversis quaestionibus 83*, however, and specifically in Question 35, that Augustine shows how the knowing of God is to be construed as that having of God in which the value of the self is realized and human happiness is attained. But we should note that, by framing his discussion of love and virtue with the references to Matthew 22:37 (the love-command) at the beginning and to John 17:3 at the end, Augustine has set the stage for the treatment of love in *De diversis quaestionibus 83* where, in association with just these verses, he will name the love of God *caritas*. It is almost as if the *De diversis* argument were specifically designed to fill in the one remaining blank in the *De moribus* discussion.

If *cupiditas* is love of things that can be lost, then *caritas* will, of course, be love of what cannot be snatched away while love continues in the enjoyment of its object (*quod manenti et fruenti amori auferri [non] potest*). It will be love of what cannot be absent while it is loved (*quae non potest deesse dum amatur*). This, Augustine now claims, will be *quod nihil est aliud habere quand nosse*, i.e., what we have precisely by knowing it (*De div. quaest. 83* 35.1). It has already become clear that Augustine discriminates between loves by distinguishing their objects, the eternal or the temporal. Here he puts the distinction between the objects in terms of the modes of our possession of them. Gold and other corporeal things are not the kind of things of which it is true that to know them is to have them; therefore we are not to love them. The things we are to love are rather those of which it *is* true that to know them is to have them (*De div. quaest. 83* 35.1).[24]

---

24. Since the eternal is incorporeal, knowing is, of course, the only mode of attaining it (see above, n. 18). Augustine here puts the stress on knowing as the mode of having this object — and not exclusively on the eternal as the object had by knowing — because he wishes to bring out certain features of what knowing-as-having will mean in the case of God.

This claim, however, immediately raises a rather complex question about the relation of having, knowing, and loving. In general, Augustine observes, it is perfectly possible for us to love what we do not have and to have what we do not love. Consequently, it makes perfect sense to ask whether it is also possible, in the case of the things that we have by knowing them, to have them without loving them. Augustine responds by pointing first to the case of persons who learn mathematics — the sort of thing we have by knowing it — for the sake of making money or for the sake of impressing others. Such persons clearly do not love mathematics, since they neither desired it for its own sake before they learned it nor enjoy it in its own right afterward.[25] It would seem, then, that we can have — i.e., know — such things and still not love them. But Augustine is not willing to let this answer stand. In the case of a good, he insists, one cannot fully *(perfecte)* have or know the thing without loving it. It is impossible to know how great a good it is without enjoying it; and we do not enjoy what we do not love. Therefore we cannot have *quod amandum est* unless we love it (*De div. quaest. 83* 35.1).

Although Augustine's argument has a rather dry and didactic cast, its import is immense. It positions him to make his culminating claim that living happily is nothing other than having the eternal by knowing it (*De div. quaest. 83* 35.2). The eternal is the one thing of which we can rightly have the confidence that it cannot be taken away from those who love it;[26] and it is also the very thing that we possess in no other way than by knowing it. Furthermore, the eternal is preeminent over all else *(omnium rerum praestantissimum)*; and we can possess it only through that feature of our own human being which makes us preeminent and distinctive ourselves, i.e., the mind

---

25. In framing his argument in this way, Augustine is making a tacit appeal to his preceding definition of love: *Nihil enim aliud est amare, quam propter se ipsam rem aliquam appetere* (*De div. quaest. 83* 35.1). At the same time, he is tacitly assimilating *fruitio* to love by construing it as the enjoyment of something *propter se ipsam* rather that, like *usus*, a referring of something to an end or purpose beyond itself. See definitions of *frui* and *uti* given in *De div. quaest. 83* 30.

26. Note the echo here of *De mor.* 1.3.5 (see above, p. 22).

(ea re qua praestantiores sumus, id est mente). Thus, in contrast to *cupiditas* which demeans the self by drawing it down to things beneath its own level of value and entangling it in emotions that disrupt its discerning of the truth, love of "what ought to be loved" realizes the value of the self, engaging what is distinctive of human being and making it the locus of human happiness. Consequently we are not, in this case, delineating a merely apparent happiness in which something, acknowledged or unacknowledged, must rub against the grain of who and what we are. This happiness resides rather at the point of intersection of Augustine's reckonings of what, on the other, is characteristically and distinctively human. That is why it represents the realization, rather than the demeaning, of the self and of its value.

It would be a mistake, however, to suppose that Augustine contracts the human to the mental or that he has in mind only an utterly intellectual affection when he speaks of love in this connection. To have something by means of the mind is to have it by knowing *(Quidquid auteme mente habetur, noscendo habetur)*; but no good is fully known which is not fully loved *(De div. quaest. 83* 35.2). Thus knowing is love's mode of having the eternal. It is not the same as love; and without love it is not even fully having or fully knowing (this is the difference between having mathematics and having the eternal). Love, then, is the wider term, wider because it engages not just the mind but the entire soul. Augustine makes the point clearly and unmistakably: *Neque ut sola mens potest cognoscere, ita et amare sola potest.* "Love is a kind of desire *(appetitus quidam)*; and we see that there is desire in the other parts of the soul" *(De div. quaest. 83* 35.2; my translation). When this desire is in conformity with mind and reason, there will be the internal peace and tranquility — as opposed to the stormy emotional fluctuations of *cupiditas* — in which we can contemplate the eternal with the mind *(De div. quaest. 83* 35.2).[27] Thus, Augustine concludes, the love of what we know by the mind is love that, properly speaking, will engage the other parts of the soul as well. It will unite

---

27. I follow O'Donovan — not Holte — in my interpretation of this passage; see *"Usus* and *Fruitio,"* 372.

the self — not the mind alone, but the entire soul — in a single, concentrated love for the eternal, for God.

"What is loved necessarily affects its lover with something of itself"; and the eternal, as the object loved, will tincture its lover with eternity (*De div. quaest. 83* 35.2). Thus the eternal, since it is not itself subject to loss through time or circumstance and since it cannot be absent so long as it is loved, differentiates a love that, in its attainment of its object, is also invulnerable to loss. It does not, therefore, afflict the soul with fear or infect it with the pathology of soul that Augustine delineates in his analysis of fear. Because this is so, it answers the human longing for happiness: it is something we can have when and for as long as it is wanted (*De beata vita* 2.11). And, in our having of it, since we are rightly confident that it cannot be snatched away, there will be no apprehensiveness to mar our happiness. The love that attains the eternal by knowing it and knows it by loving it — the love, that is, that fulfills the love-command (Matt. 22:37) and gains the eternal life that is to know the one true God and Jesus Christ whom God sent (John 17:3) — is the love that Augustines labels *caritas* or *dilectio* (*De div. quaest. 83* 35.2); and this love's enjoyment of the eternal is what he now designates the happy life, itself tinged with eternity *(ea demum beata vita, quae aeterna est)*. In *De moribus ecclesiae catholicae*, Augustine had written that to pursue God is to desire happiness, and to attain God is happiness itself (*De mor.* 1.11.18: *Secutio igitur Dei beatitatis appetitus est; consecutio authem, ipsa beatitas).* He has now shown what it is to attain God and how the attainment is happiness itself. He has defined the point at which, according to his reckoning, what genuinely affords human happiness intersects with what human beings distinctively are.

It is important, however, to make one further observation about Augustine's understanding of *caritas*. *Caritas* is opposed to *cupiditas* not only in its object and in the way it is formed by its object, but also in its social implications. Since the eternal is not something that can be lost against one's will, love of the eternal does not breed the fear of loss — nor, consequently, does it breed the desperate sense that, in order to obtain or to secure what one wants, one must eliminate the threat of others who

seek to acquire the same thing for themselves and thus pose
obstacles to one's own desires. It does not, therefore, set one
person against another. Rather, it puts the relations between
persons on a quite different footing, creating among them the
shared bond of a common love.[28] Augustine was already well
aware of this feature of love for God when, still at Cassiciacum,
he wrote the *Soliloquia*. There, after crying out that he had surely
shown that he loved wisdom alone, he goes on to ask what
bounds can possibly be set on love of such beauty. In this love,
far from finding others a threat or wishing to exclude them, he
wants as many as possible to join with him in desiring and
enjoying wisdom. The more wisdom is loved in common, the
more its lovers are linked in friendship (*Sol.* 1.13.22).

A year or so later, in the first book of *De libero arbitrio*,
Augustine makes this contrast between *cupiditas* and *caritas*
somewhat more explicit. He speaks of two kinds of people (*duo
genera . . . hominum*), each identified by its love, the one con-
sisting of lovers of eternal things and the other of lovers of
temporal things (*De lib. arb.* 1.15.31; 16.34). Clearly he is beginning to develop the notion that each love forms a society of its
own. In the case of *cupiditas*, that society is loose-jointed at best
and is sustained through the prescriptions and punishments of
the temporal law. These draw their force precisely from cupid-

---

28. It is important, in Augustine's case, to distinguish this shared
love of the eternal from the love of neighbor (as commanded in Matt.
22:39). The latter posed a conceptual difficulty. Just because of the way in
which he had sorted out his two loves — *cupiditas* as the (morally evil)
love of transitory things (which human beings are) and *caritas* as the
(morally good) love of eternal things (which human beings are not) — he
seemed to have no appropriate (i.e., morally good) form of love left over
to apply to love of neighbor. The problem was further exacerbated by the
usus-amor contrast which made "use," not love, the appropriate form of
human engagement with transitory things — and thus appeared to indicate that, if we are to love our neighbor, that love must somehow be a form
of "use." For excellent discussions of Augustine's attempts to resolve the
conceptual dilemmas he had created for himself, see O'Donovan, *The
Problem of Self-Love,* 112-36, and *"Usus* and *Fruitio."* In contrast to love of
neighbor, however, shared love of the eternal God created no such conceptual difficulties. It followed naturally from his conception of *caritas* and
served nicely to display the social dimension of the opposition of *caritas*
to *cupiditas*.

ity's fear of loss (i.e., they threaten loss to those who violate the law); and they are designed to regulate the possession of "the things which can be called 'ours' for a time when people avidly *(cupiditate)* cling to them" in such a way as to preserve peace and social order *(De lib. arb.* 1.15.32; my translation). So long as people fear the loss of these things, they will accept certain limits on their use of them; and the city — "such a city as can be composed of people of this sort" — will be maintained *(De lib. arb.* 1.15.32).

Thus a kind of social order is derived from *cupiditas,* just as from *caritas;* and it is plain that, as early as 388, Augustine was already working on lines that anticipate the well-known statement of *The City of God: Fecerunt itaque civitates duas amore duo (De civ. Dei* 14.28). In converting the question of human happiness into a question of human love, Augustine also drew its social dimension into the very heart of the matter. *Caritas,* in seeking and attaining the eternal, also unites persons in the common bond of a love shared without threat or envy; it creates a social order that is not rooted in the fear of loss.

IV

Often, I suspect, we allow ourselves to be deceived by our own translations. The words that we use to render *cupiditas* into English (or into other modern languages) — words like "passion," "lust," or "desire" — are terms that, in our own usage, we tend to distinguish from "love" and to assign to some lower, less honored, level of human feeling and emotion. They serve in particular to designate a kind of primal human sensuality or primitive desire that wells up from the depths of the psyche and lunges blindly at the objects which it would use, imperiously, to satisfy its cravings. What these terms name, therefore, is not love. At the same time, however, words such as these are the terms we employ to convey the force and power of human feeling and to register the intensity of its yearnings and its pleasures. Since we assign them to *cupiditas,* we no longer have them available for *caritas.* In consequence, *caritas* becomes a rather desiccated love, its sheer emotive force drained way by the lack of words to express it. For Augustine, furthermore, *caritas* is distinctively intertwined with mind, with reason, and with knowing (just as *cupiditas* is distinctively intertwined with fear and apprehensiveness); and contemporary habit prefers to oppose reason and emotion rather than to join them together (we must, somehow, shed our rationality in order to give emotion free and "healthy" expression). On this score too, then, we are ill-equipped with words to convey the passion of Augustine's *caritas*. The result is a reading of Augustine in which, as in Yeats's poem, the best lacks all conviction and the worst is full of passionate intensity.[29]

This reading, however, is a misreading. Augustine does not use *cupiditas* and *caritas* to distinguish lust from love; he uses them to distinguish two loves. Both count as *amor*.[30] The point is critical if we are to understand Augustine properly. *Cupiditas* is not a yielding to blind lust. It is human love seeking fulfillment — happiness — in a sphere that does not and cannot provide fulfillment, the sphere of mortal and transitory things. Since these things are subject to loss, they leave us vulnerable to loss and our love for them unavoidably tinged with fear. The social consequence, as we have seen, is that person is set against person, each perceiving the other as a threat to self; and the personal consequence is a demeaning of the self. Augustine's *cupiditas* is not mere lust. It is a rendering of the hopeless fragility and desperate outcome (both for self and for society) of love's search for fulfillment where fulfillment cannot be found. Certainly this love is flawed, morally, as "the root of all evils"; but it is to be understood, all the same, as nothing less than love: love loving the wrong thing and thus love entangled in the web of unhappiness that it has spun for itself.

Caritas, too, is a rendering of love, a love no less intensely

---

29. William Butler Yeats, "The Second Coming," in *Selected Poems and Two Plays of William Butler Yeats*, ed. M. L. Rosenthal (New York, 1962), 91.

30. The point is plain enough with regard to *caritas*. It may be worth saying again, however, that Augustine defines *cupiditas* as a love *(amor)* not only by implication (as in *Sol.* 1.11.19), but also quite explicitly (as in *De lib. arb.* 1.4.10 or *De div. quaest. 83* 33 and 35.1).

passionate than *cupiditas*. In this case, of course, love seeks fulfillment where it can be found. Its object is not subject to loss; and its love, therefore, is untouched by fear. What is distinctively human — the soul with its capacities to think, to reason, to know — is not demeaned, but brought out of its emotive subjection to lesser things and realized in its full value: knowing is the mode in which this love attains it object. And this love does not set person against person, but rather joins person with person in the common bond of a shared love for a shared object. Thus *caritas* is distinguished from *cupiditas* as love fulfilled from love unfulfilled, not by any diminishment of passion or of pleasure. In fact, just because *caritas* is love seeking and attaining the object that does afford human happiness, it would be more than strange if it lacked all intensity in its seeking and all pleasure in its attainment.

Augustine saw things otherwise. He insisted that we can know a good only if we enjoy it and that we enjoy only what we love (*De div. quaest. 83* 35.1). Changing the order slightly, we might say that love only attains (i.e., knows) the eternal — God — if it enjoys the eternal; and to enjoy something, in Augustine's view, is precisely to have present what one loves (*De mor.* 1.3.4) and to take pleasure (*voluptatem*) in it (*De div. quaest. 83* 30).[31] *Caritas*, then, is full of passionate intensity, both in its pursuit of and in its attainment of God; and it is to be set over against *cupiditas*, not on that score, but because, in enjoying its object, it does attain genuine and enduring happiness. It is love loving the right thing; and therefore, in contrast to the wounded and wounding fragility of *cupiditas*, it is love no longer scarred by fear or loss but secure in its attainment to God, who does afford happiness and who cannot — it may be confident — be taken from it.

If we do not see, then, that Augustine converted the question of happiness into a question of two *loves* — two loves differentiated, not first in the lover, but first by the loved — we

---

31. The contrast between *usus* and *fruitio* is so often stated as contrast between means and ends, as if the point were only an ordering of things in relation to each other, that the sheer pleasure, the enjoyment, in *fruitio* tends to be lost from sight.

are in danger of misconstruing what he meant both by *cupiditas* and by *caritas*;[32] and we are in danger, too, of misconstruing the cultural and theological tradition within which we still largely, if often unwittingly, delineate our own notions of human love and human happiness, for that tradition was decisively shaped by Augustine and the Augustinian view of love.

---

32. The development of Augustine's view of love did not, of course, stop here. It continued well into the later stages of his career — in particular, as he gradually substituted a version of *amor sui* for *cupiditas,* as he worked out his notion of an "ordered love" in which things to be loved are loved neither more nor less than they should be (see, e.g., *De doct. chr.* 1.27.28), as he divided ways to accommodate love of neighbor within his conceptual scheme, as he correlated his understanding of love with his understanding of grace. I think it is fair to say, however, that the lines along which these developments would take place were set in Augustine's early elaboration of the contrast beween *cupiditas* and *caritas*.

Augustine and the Hermeneutics of Love: Some Preliminary Considerations

Ernest L. Fortin

Theology is that part of religion which requires brains.
G. K. Chesterton

In a letter written at the height of the bitter Pelagian controversy, St. Jerome pays tribute to Augustine's "worldwide fame" and hails him as a man whom "Catholics revere as the second founder of the ancient faith": *In orbe celebraris, Catholici te conditorem antiquae rursum fidei uenerantur.*[1] The compliment, which is by no means unique — it would soon be echoed by others, including Possidius, Augustine's friend and biographer[2] — is all the more striking since in this instance it comes from someone whose relations with Augustine were often less than cordial. To speak of Augustine as a second founder is not to imply that his sole achievement was to restore the Christian faith to its pristine integrity at a time when it was being threatened by absorption into Roman political life on the one hand and the spread of heresy on the other. Scholars have long been divided over the

---

1. Jerome, *Letter* 141 (to Augustine), *P.L.* 22, col. 1180.
2. Cf. Possidius, *Vita Augustini,* 7 (*P.L.* 32, col. 39), where Augustine is credited with having single-handedly brought Christianity back to life in Africa.

issue of whether or not the new founding was faithful to the
spirit of the original founding, but no one ever claimed that it
was a simple return to it. How, then, do the two differ?

If one were to venture an answer to that complex question, one might be tempted to say that what primitive Christianity lacked and did not yet need was what now goes under
the name of "theology," by which I mean nothing more than
the concerted attempt to arrive at a clearer grasp of the teachings of the faith through the use of perfected reason or philosophy. It is a sign of Augustine's genius that he was the first
Latin writer to develop and carry to a high degree of perfection
— some would say to its highest degree of perfection — this
new approach to the study of the divinely revealed truth, even
if he himself never called it theology.[3] Others in his entourage,
Ambrose and Marius Victorinus among them, had begun to
move in the same direction, but their accomplishments are
meager by comparison with his.

The feat was not a mean one, especially since philosophy
was never taught as a formal discipline in the schools of the
Latin West. Any knowledge of it that one might acquire had to
come from books, and an astonishingly small number of important ones at that: those of Cicero to begin with, Cicero's version
of the *Timaeus,* Aristotle's *Categories* (for which Augustine had
little use),[4] and, beyond that, a handful of Neoplatonic texts that
had recently been translated into Latin.[5] Few authors in our
tradition have managed to do so much with so little. To this
curious state of affairs can be traced the unmistakable originality
but also the peculiar limitations of Augustine's thought. One
thing is certain: thanks to him, a new mode of knowledge, based
on love and incommensurable with anything to which the philosophical tradition was accustomed, would dominate the intellectual scene for the next thousand years or more. My intention

---

3. Augustine appears to use the word only in connection with
Varro's distinction between three kinds of theology: poetic, civil, and natural; cf. *Civ. Dei,* VI, 5. Throughout the patristic period, "theology," the
"discourse on God," is most often used in contradistinction to "economy,"
the account of God's operations in the world.

4. Cf. *Confessions,* IV, 16.

5. *Ibid.,* VII, 9.

is to take a closer look at the nature of this knowledge and then turn briefly to three problems that are more directly related to the situation that we presently face. For the sake of convenience, I shall concentrate on two of Augustine's most influential works, which happen to complement each other on this point, the *Confessions* and the treatise *On Christian Doctrine*.

I

It is interesting but not at all surprising that the passion for the truth that we associate with Augustine's intellectual activity was first kindled in his soul, not by the Bible, but by his reading of Cicero's *Hortensius* at the age of nineteen. No doubt the Bible occasionally speaks of the truth in the sense in which we normally use that term (less often perhaps than we like to think), but it cannot be said to have any real interest in it. It clearly has no use for speculation, never indulges in it, and hardly shows any awareness of it. Philosophy, the science in which the quest for speculative truth culminates, is not mentioned at all in the Hebrew Scriptures and only once in the New Testament, where it is all but equated with "empty deceit" (Col. 2:8).

Indeed, unlike other, more or less contemporary literary texts, such as the *Iliad* and the *Odyssey*, the Bible in all of its parts comes across as not only nonphilosophical but downrightly antiphilosophical. It tells stories, recounts facts, and issues commands or recommendations about the way human beings ought to live, but it does not buttress its assertions with rational arguments and frowns on anyone who would demand such arguments. It has been pointed out, not entirely in jest, that the only character to give a reason for anything in the Bible is the serpent in Genesis. The very first chapter of that book contains an implicit criticism of any and all attempts to arrive at an independent knowledge of the whole that philosophy (not the Bible) calls the "world."[6] Of all the things created by God, the sky, the

---

6. The Bible speaks not of the *cosmos* but of "heaven and earth," without any intimation that the two form a unity. It goes without saying that there is no "cosmology" as such in the Bible.

traditional symbol of that "whole," is the only one along with the human couple that is not specifically pronounced good.[7] As for the New Testament writers, whom Celsus, the first philosophic critic of Christianity, saw fit to mock as "theologizing fishermen," it is doubtful whether any of them would have made much sense of, say, the *definitio fidei* of Chalcedon, all of whose terms, with the single exception of "Jesus Christ," can be traced to a definite philosophic source.[8]

As employed by the sacred writers, "truth" is more apt to mean something like fidelity or trustworthiness.[9] To say that God is true is to proclaim that he is utterly reliable, that he does not renege on his promises, or, as we still say, that he is "true" to his word, as opposed to Satan, the "father of lies" (John 8:44) or the most untrustworthy of beings. The constant teaching of the Bible is that one "knows" God to the extent that one places one's trust in him and does his will. Christ's prayer, "This is eternal life, that they know thee the only true God, and Jesus Christ whom thou hast sent" (John 17:3), is an invitation, not to develop a natural theology, but to love and obey God. In like manner, when Christ tells his disciples that "the truth will make [them] free" (John 8:32), he is not thinking primarily of freedom from error or from the opinions of the multitude, which is what philosophers strive for, but of freedom from sin. Granted, the Bible cannot help raising an implicit claim to truth insofar as it excludes every way of life other than its own, but it never engages in a rigorous discourse the aim of which would be to demonstrate by means of logical arguments the superiority of that way of life.

---

7. See on this subject the penetrating remarks by L. Strauss, *Jerusalem and Athens* (New York, 1967), and "On the Interpretation of Genesis," *L'Homme* 21/1 (1981), 5-20. That man or "Adam" is not called "good" except implicitly through his inclusion in the whole of creation is not surprising in view of what we learn about him in Genesis 2.

8. For further details, cf. E. L. Fortin, "The *Definitio Fidei* of Chalcedon and Its Philosophical Sources," *Studia Patristica* 5 (Berlin, 1962), 489-98.

9. The OT term for "truth," *emet*, which is frequently translated by *aletheia* in the NT, is derived from a root conveying the notion of firmness. For the biblical uses of these two words, cf. G. Kittel, ed., *Theological Dictionary of the New Testament*, Vol. 1 (Grand Rapids, 1964), 232-47.

This is not to assert that the Christian tradition, as distinct from the New Testament, is indifferent to or unconcerned with the truth — far from it. The biblical God may be short of "ideas," but theologians have usually been more than willing to supply what he lacks in this respect. The reason is that Christianity first comes to sight as a nonpolitical religion or as "sound doctrine" (I Tim. 1:10; Tit. 1:9; 2:1) rather than as a God-given law. In the absence of any divinely mandated legal and social system, unity was secured by a commonality of belief. Henceforth, one would be justified, not by the performance of lawful deeds, but by faith. Accordingly, no other religious tradition has ever placed a greater premium on purity of doctrine or been so much on its guard against heresy. It is no accident that the internal history of Christianity, in contrast to that of either Judaism or Islam, is dominated by theological rather than juridical disputes. Orthodoxy was thought to be more important than orthopraxy and what one held as a believer took precedence over any of the political or legal arrangements by which human beings are wont to order their temporal lives. There would thus appear to be something in the nature of the Christian revelation that renders theological speculation indispensable in the long run. My point is that this speculation is not indigenous to or expressly demanded by the New Testament itself.

The *Hortensius,* Cicero's protreptic or "exhortation" *(hortatio)* to philosophy, presented a startlingly different picture. It held up the theoretical life as the highest human possibility and the philosopher himself as the highest human type. It thereby made a young and avid Augustine, who had more than his share of riot and high summer in the blood and for whom the familiar *cursus honorum* was the mandatory road to success, aware of the fact that one's whole life could be actuated, not by the love of pleasure, honor, or any of the other worldly goods to which the vast majority of human beings are drawn, but by that most unusual of all passions — a passion so rare that few people recognize it when they come face to face with it — the passion for the truth. From that moment forward, Augustine would have no more pressing ambition. Even his early and, in retrospect, implausible nine-year flirtation with Manichaeanism is explained only by the fact that it promised a rational solution to his nagging intellectual perplexities.

The failed experiment with Manichaeanism was followed, as we know, by a period of skepticism during which, unable to conceive of an incorporeal being and hence in doubt about the very possibility of science, Augustine despaired of ever attaining his coveted goal. The last obstacle was removed when, having been introduced to the "works of the Platonists" by his friends in Milan, he discovered the world of ideas and learned of the existence of a spiritual substance on which all other substances depend.[10] The event, dramatic as it was, nevertheless turned out to be only the penultimate step in a process that reached its high point with his even more dramatic conversion to Christianity. The question is, What made this ultimate step necessary? Where exactly was Platonic philosophy at fault? Why is it that, having at last found what he was looking for, Augustine was dissatisfied with it and compelled to search for something else? What finally convinced him that happiness was not to be sought in philosophic contemplation, but in the Christian ideal of the love of God and neighbor?

Augustine's works contain a variety of answers to that question but none more readily intelligible than his probing analysis of the internal difficulties besetting classical moral and political philosophy. Stated in simplest terms, the argument runs as follows. The pagan philosophers correctly define happiness in terms of virtue or excellence, that is to say, in terms of the highest goals to which human beings can aspire, but they are unable to show the way to those goals. People are happy when they are at one with themselves and with one another, and they achieve this harmony when justice prevails both within and among them. Yet experience demonstrates that few of them ever manage to live perfectly just lives. According to Aristotle, who speaks for the tradition in this regard, justice is the disposition that inclines us to seek the good of others and, if need be, to sacrifice ourselves for their benefit.[11] This means concretely that I must be prepared to give up what I have or

---

10. *Conf.*, VII, 9.
11. Aristotle, *Nic. Ethics*, V, 1134b6 and 10.

can acquire so that someone else who also wants it may be able to enjoy it instead of me. It is unrealistic to think that people will comply with such a demand as a matter of course. By reason of their bodily nature, human beings are necessarily attached to what belongs to them as individuals and, when conflicts of interest arise, almost always prefer themselves to others. The love of their own cannot be eradicated from their souls and, in virtually all cases, proves stronger than their love of the true or the beautiful. To make matters worse, less than perfect laws combine with bad inclination and tyrannical habit to prevent them from becoming true lovers of justice. To this problem the pagan philosophers could offer no solution. They were right in stressing the need for virtue but could not secure its performance. They themselves were the first to admit that their model of the most desirable society cannot be translated into action. It exists in speech or "private discussion" only.[12] *De facto,* one is always faced with some sort of trade-off, that is to say, with a choice among a variety of regimes none of which is superior in every respect to any of the others. Even the mixed regime, which these philosophers present as the "practically" best solution to the problem, is nothing but an attempt to maximize the advantages and minimize the disadvantages of each individual regime.

Augustine's critique, which is all the more pertinent since it is based on his opponents' own principles, reminds us of the one that would later be developed by Machiavelli and his followers, who likewise took issue with classical thought on the ground of its impracticality. The difference is that Augustine never thought of lowering the standards of human behavior in order to enhance their effectiveness, as did the early modern philosophers when they boldly tried to root all moral principles in some powerful but selfish passion, such as the desire for self-preservation. If anything, his own standards are even more

12. Augustine, *Letter* 91.4. The allusion is to Plato, *Republic,* 592b, which Augustine knew indirectly through Cicero's *De Republica.* The same argument is developed at considerable length in *De Uera Religione,* I,1–VI,11, and in the *City of God,* II,21, and XIX,21, apropos of Cicero's definition of the city, which in Augustine's view applies to Rome only on condition that the reference to justice be deleted from it.

stringent than the most stringent standards of the classical tradition. As he saw it, pagan philosophy was bound to fail, not because it made unreasonable demands on human nature, but because its proponents did not know or were unwilling to apply the proper remedy to its congenital weakness. That remedy consists in following Christ, apart from whom one can do nothing (cf. John 15:5), for he alone both reveals the true goal of human existence and furnishes the means whereby it may be attained.

Underlying this whole argument is the view that the knowledge vouchsafed to us through divine revelation differs not only in degree of certitude but in kind from all other forms of knowledge. It is a salutary or beatifying knowledge — *rerum diuinarum atque salubrium scientia*[13] — one that calls for a decision on the part of the knower and is inseparable from the love of God and neighbor. In and of itself it has the power to transform the individual who apprehends it, and it is fully appropriated only when it issues in those deeds to which it points as its fulfillment. Its object is unique in that it cannot be known unless it is also loved. As such, it represents the good, not of the intellect alone but of the whole person, and thus carries with it the guarantee of happiness. As Augustine puts it elsewhere, anyone who is "taught of God" (Isa. 54:13; John 6:45) has been given simultaneously both "to know what he ought to do and to do what he knows";[14] he not only "has the power to come but does come";[15] he not only "believes what ought to be loved but loves what he believes."[16] Of no other truth can it be said that it is intrinsically efficacious or, in one and the same act, both theoretical and practical. Between theory and practice there is in all ordinary cases a hiatus that can only be overcome by an act of the will, which philosophers are reluctant to make until such time as the necessary evidence is at hand. In classical philosophy, some disciplines — grammar, logic, or medicine,

---

13. *De Doctrina Christiana*, IV.5, 7.

14. Augustine, *De Gratia Christi*, 13,14, P.L. 44, col. 367.

15. *Ibid.*, 14,15, col. 368.

16. *Ibid.*, 12,13, col. 367. It is precisely because the word of God is spoken with power (cf. I Cor. 2:4-5) that anyone who resists it is guilty of sin.

for example — were considered to be both sciences and arts, but only insofar as their practitioners were engaged in different acts at different moments. Yet this is not so in the present case, where the two formalities are bound together in such a way as to be inconceivable one without the other.

The foregoing remarks are corroborated in unexpected fashion by the discussion of the task of the Christian orator in Book IV of *De Doctrina Christiana*. That task is said to comprise three parts, which are none other than the ones listed in Cicero's rhetorical treatises: to teach *(docere)*, to please *(delectare)*, and to move or persuade *(flectere)*.[17] What scholars usually fail to note is that Augustine's treatment of this subject is anything but a simple rehash of the Ciceronian theory. We learn among other things that the Christian orator's preeminent function is not to persuade, as it is for Cicero's orator, but to teach. Moreover, the teaching in which he engages is not a matter of narrating in as plausible a way as possible the facts of the case, as any lawyer or political orator must begin by doing; it consists in imparting a "doctrine" in the strictest sense of the word, one whose truth cannot be called into question because it rests on the authority of God himself. Finally, the Christian orator does not have to use passion as a middle term in order to secure the assent of his listeners or resort to any of the adornments on which other orators rely for their success. Nothing of course prevents him from speaking persuasively and in a pleasing manner if he has the ability to do so, for he has nothing to gain by boring his audience. Indeed, it would be a shame if error were to be clothed in attractive garb by its proponents while truth were made to appear tedious for lack of proper embellishments. The fact remains that the divine truth is persuasive in its own right and does not owe its efficacy to the rhetorical prowess of the speaker.

It follows as a necessary consequence that, unlike his pagan counterpart, Augustine's orator must avoid lies at all costs, even the most harmless ones, lest by indulging in them

---

17. *De Doctrina Christiana,* IV,12. See, for a fuller treatment, E. L. Fortin, "Augustine and the Problem of Christian Rhetoric," *Augustinian Studies* 5 (1974), 85-100.

he should be suspected of lying about the Christian message itself and undermine his own credibility. He may know vastly *more* than his less learned hearers and is thus often compelled to adapt himself to their limited intellectual capacities, but what he knows is not something *other* than what every Christian knows or should know. There is finally only one truth, "which all hear in the same measure when it is publicly spoken, but which each one appropriates in his own measure."[18] Never is there any question of persuading the hearer to accept a doctrine to which the speaker has not previously given his wholehearted assent. What one knows in one way "in the world at large" is not essentially different from what one knows "in the privacy of one's chambers."[19] The same cannot be said of Cicero's orator, who starts from the premise that human beings are vastly unequal in regard to intellectual capacity and will always prefer a plausible lie to an implausible truth.

It should be clear by now that the type of knowledge Augustine has in mind bears little resemblance to what he refers to as the "heartless doctrines" — *doctrinae sine corde* — of the philosophers, doctrines that he knew only too well since they are the ones in which, up to the time of their conversion, he and his friend Alypius had been entangled.[20] The problem with the philosopher is that he is too proud to acknowledge that his salvation could come from anyone but himself. This self-congratulatory or self-idolizing posture is at the root of his seeming condescension toward the multitude. Philosophers parade as lovers and teachers of moral virtue, but not one of them appears to have been eager to place the service of his fellow human beings above his own good. Their model is Socrates, whose aloofness from the affairs of the city is a better index of his fundamental disposition than his public declarations of piety or his professed concern for the welfare of Athens.[21] If

---

18. Augustine, *Tractatus in Joan.*, 98,2, *P.L.* 25, col. 1881.

19. *Ibid.*, 98,6.

20. Cf. *Confessions,* VIII,8.

21. See especially the subtle analysis of Socrates's relationship to Athens in Plato's *Apology of Socrates,* which makes it clear that the philosopher lives in the city as someone who is not at home in it and does not really belong to it. For an interpretation of the *Apology* along the lines

Socrates can boast of his ignorance, it is not because he is humble but because he has learned what true knowledge is and can distinguish it from its opposite. His would-be ignorance is the obverse of a deep-seated pride that causes him to distance himself from the rest of society. He speaks to his judges as one speaks to children, telling them only what is good for them, regardless of whether it is true or not.[22] His own public speeches were meant to be more "persuasive" than genuinely truthful. They were aimed as much at keeping the multitude away from the truth as they were at attracting to it the few who had proved themselves worthy of it by their ability to penetrate the disguise in which it is habitually cloaked.

Philosophers follow their personal bent, associating with their own kind and mingling with others only as necessity dictates. A gulf separates their arrogance *(praesumptio)* from the humble "confession" of the believer.[23] Bridging that gulf is not an easy matter, as we know from the moving story of the philosopher Marius Victorinus, Augustine's older contemporary, who had converted to Christianity but, under pretense that walls do not make Christians, refused for a long time to be seen in church for fear of alienating his pagan friends.[24]

As was suggested earlier, the truth to which Augustine directs our attention is a truth whose object cannot be grasped unless it is also loved. This is not to be understood to mean that the object in question does not *exist* unless it is loved or that it is a simple projection of one's hopes and desires. It is nonetheless inevitable that sooner or later questions should be raised about its cognitive status. Augustine himself grounded his position in the biblical notion that human beings are created in the image of God. The argument assumes that the process by which a finite being attains its perfection takes the form of a

suggested here, cf. L. Strauss, "On Plato's *Apology of Socrates* and *Crito,*" in T. L. Pangle, ed., *Studies in Platonic Political Philosophy* (Chicago and London, 1983), 38-66; G. Anastaplo, "Human Being and Citizen: A Beginning to the Study of Plato's *Apology of Socrates,*" in J. Cropsey, ed., *Ancients and Moderns* (New York and London, 1964), 16-49.

22. Cf. *Apol. of Socrates,* 39c ff.
23. *Ibid.,* VII,20.
24. *Ibid.,* VIII,2.

return to its principle. Hence the familiar *a te–ad te* tandem that structures the whole of the *Confessions*.[25] Human beings come from God and their hearts are not at peace until they find their rest in him. But then one cannot love God without loving those whom God loves, and God loves all his creatures. This is what Augustine did not find in the books of the Platonists, however much he may have felt indebted to them for other reasons. By their pride, philosophers enshrine disunity among human beings. The knowledge in which they traffic is essentially divisive and forecloses any return to the unity and wholeness for which everyone consciously or unconsciously yearns.

II

Against the background of these remarks and in an effort to lend greater concreteness to them, it may be in our interest to glance at three specific issues in regard to which Augustine's concerns intersect in one way or another with those of our time. The first has to do with the Augustinian notion of love and friendship, particularly as it affects the life of society as a whole. As is well known, the model from which Augustine works is supplied by Acts 4:32, which extols the harmony that characterized the life of the earliest Christian community, all of whose members are said to have been "of one heart and soul." Until fairly recently, no one had noticed or paid much attention to the fact that Augustine frequently adds to that statement the words *in Deum*, "bent" or "intent on God." The addition, which is clearly deliberate — it occurs in thirty-one of the forty-two instances in which the verse is quoted[26] — tells us a great deal

---

25. This explains, among other things, the peculiar structure of the *Confessions*, which begins with an account of Augustine's spiritual odyssey (Bks. I-IX), ends with a commentary on the first chapter of Genesis (Bks. XI-XIII), and unites the two apparently disparate parts by means of Book X, which is devoted to an analysis of memory, the intellectual faculty by means of which one uncovers the presence of God within oneself and begins one's ascent toward him.

26. Cf. T. J. van Bavel, "*Ante omnia* et *in Deum* dans la *Regula Sancti Augustini*," *Vigiliae Christianae* 12 (1958), 157-65.

about Augustine's understanding of the relationship that binds people together as friends and fellow citizens. It makes it clear that human beings become one not by looking at one another, but by looking together in the direction of something outside of and higher than themselves. Any deep and lasting relationship presupposes a common good of some sort in which the parties involved can communicate and which serves as the ground of their unity. This relationship rests ultimately on God, the supreme good, the love of which is implied in the love of any lesser good that one may wish to pursue.

Our contemporaries usually have little patience with this line of inquiry and are more likely to think of friendship in terms of what is now called an "I-Thou" relationship. As the use of such unnatural words as "I" and "Thou" reveals, however, the new understanding is the product of a process whereby one prescinds from the actual end or ends to which individuals or communities are dedicated. It presumes that there are no pre-established, naturally knowable, or divinely ordained ends in the attainment of which human beings find their perfection, and it dismisses as meaningless any talk of such ends.

Little wonder, then, that our modern sensibilities should be offended by the famous teaching of *De Doctrina Christiana* which stipulates that God is to be "enjoyed" or loved for his own sake, whereas everything else, including all other human beings, is to be "used" or loved only as a means to that end;[27] for such a view would seem to reflect a purely instrumental conception of human love and friendship. Scholars have even asked whether Augustine himself, who omits any mention of this distinction in his later works, had not developed second thoughts about it, even though no such change of heart is recorded in the *Retractationes*.[28] However, a simpler explanation may be that, in accordance with a method of procedure in-

---

27. *De Doctrina Christiana,* I,22.

28. Cf. O. O'Donovan, *The Problem of Self-Love in St. Augustine* (New Haven and London, 1980), who calls Augustine's discussion of this matter in Bk. I of the *De Doctrina Christiana* a "false step" and notes that "there is not one single instance in any later writing of the verb *uti* being used of the love of men for other men" (p. 29).

herited from the Platonic school, Augustine tends to study all
things in the light of their highest principles and that this tendency is what leads to the extreme formulations for which he
is notorious.

Properly understood, the distinction between "enjoyment" *(frui)* and "use" *(uti)* directs our attention to one of the
most problematic features of the New Testament teaching on
love, to say nothing of the modern account of love and friendship as "I-Thou" relationships. It is characteristic of the New
Testament commandment of universal love that it ignores all
the limitations that nature imposes on us in this matter. One is
summoned to love others without discrimination and independently of their personal merits or qualities. But this could
amount to little more than a tyranny of every individual over
every other individual. The pitfall is avoided only if the love
that unites human beings has its ground in the one good that
can be shared by all of them without partition or diminution,
namely, God himself.

It might be added, also in Augustine's defense, that his
understanding of love has nothing of the sentimentality that
attaches to this notion in the modern mind. No one who has
reflected on the role of *disciplina* in Augustine's thought will
have the slightest doubt about that. Augustine was all for per-
suasion when it could be used to good effect, but he knew its
limits for having experienced them himself. Even his famous
maxim, "Love and do what you will," seems to have had a
much tougher meaning than the one that is now commonly
attributed to it. It belongs to the context of the Donatist controversy and refers to the harsh treatment to which Augustine's
disciples were compelled to resort in order to bring the adversary to his senses. The message was clear: one could deal with
the intractable Donatists as the necessities of the case required,
so long as one remembered to love them.[29]

My second set of remarks concerns the familiar charge that
Augustine inherited from his Neoplatonic mentors a tendency

---

29. See on this subject J. Gallay, "*Dilige et quod uis fac*: notes d'exégèse
augustinienne," *Recherches de science religieuse* 43 (1955), 545-55.

to deprecate human values; a negative view of the body and everything connected with it; an otherworldly or escapist outlook at odds with the spirit of the gospel; and a severity in moral matters that has justifiably earned him a place among the great rigorists of all times. There are any number of statements in the Augustinian corpus from which such an impression might be gained, but here again one wonders whether the complaints are due less to any flaw in Augustine's thought than to our present inability to penetrate beneath the surface of his writings to the substance of that thought.

First of all, it is too easy to attribute to Plato and the Platonic tradition generally the blend of intemperate spiritualism and dire pessimism in regard to worldly matters for which they are often blamed by modern scholars. Even the *Phaedo*, the Platonic dialogue most open to this kind of misinterpretation, conveys a markedly different teaching. It sets forth two views that are in obvious tension with each other: one that perceives the body as an impediment to the soul, a prison from which the latter must escape if it is to regain the freedom necessary for the exercise of its own operations, and one that stresses the contribution which the bodily senses make to the life of the soul by awakening it gradually to its true nature, thus making possible its ascent from the sensible world to the suprasensible world of ideas. By so doing, Platonism does not offer a distorted picture of human life; it merely respects its complexity by showing how human beings are constantly being pulled in opposite directions by a dual nature whose diverse needs are reconcilable only with the greatest difficulty.

Moreover, by the time of Plotinus and Porphyry, the old body-prison analogy had already been profoundly revised if not actually abandoned in favor of a novel theory which can be described in round terms as that of the hypostatic union of body and soul and which emphasizes to a far greater degree than Plato had done the essential unity of the human being. Body and soul were not two co-substantial principles out of which the human being was compounded — on that point the Neoplatonists remained steadfast in their opposition to Aristotle's hylomorphic theory — but two substances, each one complete in its own right, which mysteriously came together, like sunlight and air or fire and iron, so as to form a single being without merging into each other or losing their respective identities. The new theory, which interestingly enough is best known to us from one of Augustine's letters,[30] proved valuable in other ways as well. Via Leo the Great's *Tome,* which follows Augustine closely, this new theory served as the model for the account that the Council of Chalcedon would soon be giving of the "unconfused union" of the divine and human natures in the single person of Christ. Nor does the theory make only a belated appearance in Augustine's works, as its presence in *Letter* 137 might seem to suggest; for it has recently been shown that the same conception is already operative in his early dialogues.[31]

The difference between Augustine and most present-day philosophers and theologians is not that the latter have a better grasp of the role of the body in human life or that they hold human and artistic values in higher esteem; it lies rather in the fact that Augustine was intent on preserving or restoring human wholeness by directing all of the individual's activities

---

30. Augustine, *Letter* 137,11:

Some insist upon being furnished with an explanation of the manner in which the Godhead was so united with a human soul and body as to constitute the one person of Christ, when it was necessary that this should be done once in the world's history, with as much boldness as if they were themselves able to furnish an explanation of the manner in which the soul is so united to the body as to constitute the one person of man, an event which is occurring every day. For just as the soul is united to the body in one person so as to constitute a man, in the same way is God united to man so as to constitute Christ. In the former personality there is a combination of soul and body; in the latter there is a combination of the Godhead and man. Let my reader, however, guard against borrowing his idea from the properties of material bodies, by which two fluids when combined are so mixed that neither preserves its original character; although even among material bodies there are exceptions, such as light, which sustains no change when combined with the atmosphere. . . .

31. Cf. G. Madec, "Le spiritualisme augustinien à la lumière du *De Immortalitate Animae, "L'Opera letteraria di Agostino tra Cassiciacum e Milano* (Palermo, 1987), 179-90.

to the goal or goals to which they are intrinsically ordered. There are few more vivid accounts anywhere in Christian literature of the manner in which the soul rises "step by step" from the delights afforded by the bodily senses to the inner contemplation of the wisdom from which these and all other delights derive than the celebrated "vision of Ostia" in Book IX of the *Confessions*. As a follower of those philosophers who, in his words, had come closest to Christianity, Augustine knew not only that love takes many forms but that there is gradual progression from the lower of these to the higher and that, in life as we know it, the latter continue to be supported by the former. Never is there any question of repressing the lower forms so that the higher ones might emerge through what has since been reinterpreted as a process of sublimation. To quote Augustine himself, "Cupidity must not be removed but transformed": *non auferatur cupiditas sed mutetur*. Love must be given the opportunity to "migrate" from the creature, by which it is held bound, to the creator: *Amor tuus migret: rumpe funes a creatura, alliga ad creatorem.*[32] The experience of the inadequacy of the objects to which it is first attracted, rather than the forced abandonment of these objects as a result of the pressures that society brings to bear on us, is what causes the soul to redirect its energies toward more noble or more suitable objects. This accounts for the astonishingly erotic images used in *Soliloquies*, I.13, 22, for example, to describe something as ethereal as the love of wisdom:

> REASON: Now, we are trying to discover what kind of a lover of wisdom you are: that wisdom which you desire to behold and to possess with purest gaze and embrace, with no veil between and, as it were, naked, such as wisdom allows to very few and these the most chosen of its lovers. If you were inflamed with the love of some beautiful woman, would she not rightly refuse to give herself to you if she discovered that you loved anything but herself? And will the purest beauty of wisdom reveal itself to you unless you burn for it alone?

---

32. Augustine, *Sermo Denis* XIV, in *Miscellanea Agostiniana*, I (Rome, 1930), 66-67.

AUGUSTINE: Why, then, am I unhappily held back and why am
I delayed by this wretched torture? Surely, I have shown that I
have nothing else, since that which is not loved for itself is not
really loved. I do love wisdom alone and for its own sake, and
it is on account of wisdom that I want to have or fear to be
without other things, such as life, tranquillity, and my friends.
What limit can there be to my love of that Beauty, in which I do
not only not begrudge it to others, but I even look for many who
will long for it with me, sigh for it with me, possess it with me,
enjoy it with me; they will be all the dearer to me the more we
share that love in common.[33]

In all of this there is no Rousseauean or Freudian attempt
to derive the higher from the lower, if only because Augustine
did not have any doubts about the preexistence of the higher
as an independent object of desire. Nothing was more foreign
to his mind than the modern scientific view which denies that
there is in the human soul a yearning for the eternal, looks upon
love as an "artificial" and, down deep, selfish feeling born of
the repression of the sexual appetite,[34] and rules out *a priori* any

33. Th. Gilligan transl., *Writings of St. Augustine,* Vol. 1, The Fathers
of the Church (Washington, 1948), 372-73.

34. Cf. J. J. Rousseau, *Emile,* Bk. IV, A. Bloom transl. (New York,
1979), esp. p. 329: "And what is true love itself if it is not chimera, lie, and
illusion? We love the image we make for ourselves far more than we love
the object to which we apply it. If we saw what we love exactly, there
would be no more love on earth." Cf. *Discourse on the Origin and Foundations
of Inequality,* R. Masters, ed., J. J. Rousseau, *The First and Second Discourses*
(New York, 1964), 135. Also Kant, *Conjectural Beginning of Human History,*
who, pursuing Rousseau's line of thought, writes:

Next to the instinct for food, by means of which nature preserves
the individual, the greatest prominence belongs to the sexual instinct, by means of which she preserves the species. Reason, once
aroused, did not delay in demonstrating its influence here as well.
In the case of animals, sexual attraction is merely a matter of transient, mostly episodic impulse. But man soon discovered that for
him this attraction can be prolonged and even increased by means
of the imagination — a power that carries on its business, to be sure,
the more moderately, but at once also the more constantly and
uniformly, the more its object is removed from the senses. By means
of the imagination, he discovered, the surfeit was avoided which
goes with the satisfaction of mere animal desire. The fig leaf, then,

moral, intellectual, and religious conversion of the kind that Augustine underwent. If, as Augustine thought, the soul has its own natural order, and if that order can be restored through the convergence of wisdom, intellect, and love, there is no point in trying to reconstruct it on the basis of some materialistic or deterministic conception of nature. The famous dichotomies about which one hears so much nowadays, such as the irreducible opposition between duty and inclination, or between the individual and society, or between the pursuit of one's own good and the good of others, belong to the context of modern thought, not to that of Augustine's thought. One can read the whole of Augustine and never have the impression of being in the presence of a man who only pretends to love what he really hates.

My last series of comments focuses on the so-called hermeneutical problem as it arises in the first three books of the *De Doctrina Christiana*, the only work in all of patristic literature devoted in its entirety to this topic. The matter is of considerable theoretical and practical interest, especially in view of the innumerable controversies to which we have lately been treated concerning the possibility of interpretation. Currently the most fashionable theory is the one that denies that possibility. Texts would have no meaning independent of the activity of the interpreter, who cannot help injecting his own perspective into them. In Morris Zapp's memorable words, "Every decoding is another encoding." Everything is interpretation, which is as

---

was a far greater manifestation of reason than that shown in the earlier stage of development. . . . *Refusal* was the feat that brought about the passage from the merely sensual to spiritual attractions, from mere animal desire gradually to love, and along with this from the feeling of the merely agreeable to a taste for beauty, at first only for beauty in man but at length for beauty in nature as well. In addition, there came a first hint of the development of man as a moral creature. This came from the sense of decency, which is an inclination to inspire others to respect by proper manners, i.e., by concealing all that which might arouse low esteem. Here, incidentally, lies the real basis of all true sociability." (Kant, *On History*, L. W. Beck, ed. [Indianapolis, 1963], 56-57)

much as to say that nothing is interpretation, as Nietzsche, the grandfather of our present-day deconstructionists, taught us more than a century ago; for all interpretation is necessarily interpretation in the light of something that is not itself subject to interpretation.

Faced with the task of explaining a text, the interpreter cannot be content with merely repeating the author's own words since in that case we should never know whether he has understood anything or not. This leaves him with no other choice but to explain the text in his own words, a perilous enterprise that inevitably leads to a subtle distortion of the author's meaning. To restate the problem in terms of the narrower hermeneutical circle in which every interpreter is supposedly trapped: one can only understand the part in relation to the whole, which is known to us only through its individual parts. There is, in short, no such thing as a presuppositionless interpretation. This implies that there is no preexisting text, either, not even for the author himself, whose work is always fraught with a variety of meanings of which he is not himself aware. In consequence, the old rule of thumb according to which the first task of the interpreter is to try to understand the author as he understood himself loses its *raison d'etre*, based as it is on the naive assumption that there is "text" to begin with.

The same observations would apply to the Bible, whose meaning is not one but indefinitely many and which can thus be said to lack any determinate or permanent meaning. Words and sentences can obviously be taken in a variety of senses — literal, allegorical, ironic, or whatever it may be — and any text can contain more than one meaning, all of them intended by the author for the same or for different audiences. But a text that has an indefinite number of meanings has no meaning at all. It can confirm us in our prejudices, inasmuch as what we find in it is barely more than what we bring to it, but it cannot liberate us from those prejudices. Instead of a new world, our new Christopher Columbus always ends up by discovering Genoa. What was intended by Nietzsche as an appeal to creativity, the purpose of which was to rescue the modern herd animal from the abyss of mediocrity into which he was about to sink, has instead become an instrument of liberalism. Since there are no authoritative interpretations anywhere and no authoritative texts to interpret, one is free to think and act as one sees fit, as long as one does not interfere with anyone else's freedom.

As might be expected, *De Doctrina Christiana* takes a different tack. It begins with a synopsis of the rules of faith and conduct by which Christians are to be guided in their reading of the sacred text.[35] The rule of faith includes such doctrines as those pertaining to the triune God and his attributes, Christ and his redemptive work, the Church as the body of Christ, and the last things or life after death. As for Christianity's moral teaching, it is summed up in the dual precept of the love of God and neighbor, the alpha and the omega of divine revelation. The whole of the Bible is in fact geared to the inculcation of this supreme commandment, so much so that anyone who has grasped it can dispense with Scripture altogether.

The logical difficulty in the present case is that we are not told how one arrives at a knowledge of the truths that are then called into play as rules of faith or of conduct. It does not suffice to say that one depends on the church for this information, for the same problem arises in connection with the foundation of that authority: one knows that the church can be trusted because its authority is vouched for by the Bible, and, conversely, one knows that the Bible can be trusted because its authority is vouched for by the church. The problem is alluded to by Augustine himself, who points out that there are two matters to be treated in his book, "things" and "signs."[36] By "things" he means in the first instance the basic truths that have just been presented in capsule form, and by "signs" the words used to express them. But he also says that "things are learned by signs" — *res per signa discuntur* (I.2, 2) — at which point the argument again appears to beg the question: signs are interpreted in the light of things, which are themselves known only by means of these signs. Nothing, it seems, has been accomplished. A vicious circle similar to the one that plagues modern

---

35. Similar synopses are to be found at the beginning of *De Agone Christiano* and *Enchiridion*.
36. *De Doctrina Christiana*, I.2,2.

hermeneutics is apparently at work in the Augustinian scheme
as well.

One might reply, first of all, that Augustine was not acquainted with the problem of interpretation in the precise form
in which it would pose itself in our century and hence cannot
be faulted for not dealing with it thematically; and, secondly,
that *De Doctrina Christiana* is an emphatically Christian book,
that is, a book written by a Christian for other Christians —
above all for Christian preachers, who were presumed to be
familiar with the teachings of the faith, to be wholly committed
to them, and to require no further proof of their truth. Does this
mean that his treatment of this subject is inadequate and that
he has less to teach us about it than any of those who have since
written on it? Not necessarily.

It is significant that Augustine broaches the question of
interpretation proper only in Book II, which is limited to a
discussion of such external aids to the understanding of the
Scriptures as may be provided by the study of grammar, history, the natural and mathematical sciences, and dialectic. It is
only in Book III, which tackles the thornier issue of how one
goes about making sense of the obscure passages of Scripture,
that actual rules of interpretation, some of them borrowed
from the Donatist Tyconius, are offered. We are given to understand that, contrary to what is often taken for granted
today, there is no such thing as a universal hermeneutics and
no necessity for it. Specific rules of interpretation are required
only when the text is not clear and needs to be deciphered. I
do not have to be well versed in hermeneutical theory to read
the local newspaper, however slanted its reporting may be,
and I can be reasonably certain that its unintelligible passages,
if there are any, are due to some editorial lapse or typesetting
error, in which case rules of interpretation would be useless
anyway.

The tacit premise of modern biblical hermeneutics, as it
developed in the seventeenth century, is that the Bible is unintelligible on its own terms and is therefore in need of a complex
exegetical method that allows us to understand its individual
parts in terms of their genesis or the personal agenda of their
respective authors. Spinoza, the first great philosophical ex-

ponent of that method,[37] denied that there is any speculative teaching to be extracted from the sacred text and reduced its moral teaching to two virtues, justice and charity, redefined and simplified in such a way as to support his own political program. Both are rooted in the desire for self-preservation and neither one bears any relationship to the various other moral virtues by which human beings are perfected in themselves. The argument in a nutshell is that the Bible is not the work of a single divine author, that its various parts do not cohere with one another, and that one ought to read it as one would read any other book, that is, in the light of such information as is accessible to the unaided human reason.

Augustine starts from the opposite premise. He assumes that, as a divinely inspired book, the Bible is in principle intelligible from beginning to end. To be sure, some of its parts are obscure, but the obscurities are deliberate. God has willed them as a means of arousing the curiosity of the reader, of sustaining his interest, and of keeping him humble. On this score Augustine is in full agreement with Tyconius, although unlike Tyconius he is not at all confident that the application of the proper rules will eventually dispose of all the obscurities. The matter is of little practical consequence since we know beforehand that the teaching of the clear passages cannot be contradicted by that of the obscure passages, whatever it may be, the reason being that a benevolent God would never lead his followers astray or deprive them of any necessary aid to their salvation.

Few contemporary biblical scholars are inclined to pay much attention to Augustine's hermeneutical theory. Still, it is permissible to ask whether, as practitioners of a discipline that is not known for its propensity to reflect on its own presuppositions, they might not find it to their advantage to give more serious thought to it. Nobody denies the enormous contribution that modern scholarship has made to our understanding of the Bible. The only question concerns the level of that contribution and the criteria in the light of which its worth is best

---

37. The crucial text is that of the *Theologico-Political Treatise,* Ch. 7: "On the Interpretation of Scripture."

assessed. The question is not an easy one to answer, but the fact that it is again being raised is a sign that a few of our contemporaries are no longer as sure as they once were of the adequacy, let alone the ultimate superiority, of the modern hermeneutical framework.

I began by suggesting, somewhat timidly, that Augustine's thought suffers from certain liabilities that are attributable, at least in part, to the scarcity or the incompleteness of the philosophical materials with which he had to work. What the mystical Platonism with which he came into contact lacked most conspicuously was a fully developed notion of nature. When asked by his interlocutor, personified Reason, to state in a single sentence all that he wants to know, the Augustine of the *Soliloquies* replies: "God and the soul, nothing more!"[38] Nowhere in the tradition within which Augustine works does one find a *bona fide* science of nature or, unless I am mistaken, a single treatise *Peri Physeos*. The matter proved to be of some consequence for the evolution of Christian theology. On the basis of the distinction between "things" and "signs," Augustine's medieval disciples were inclined to view the world, not as something that had its own internal consistency and intelligibility, but rather as an elaborate system of symbols, an enchanted forest as it were, in which every tree, flower, or other natural object functions as a reminder of an invisible reality far more beautiful than anything the eye has ever seen.

The problem — and it is not unlike the one we ran into when we examined Augustine's theory of interpretation — is that in order to recognize a sign for what it is one has to have some knowledge, however vague, of the reality that it signifies. In the Augustinian tradition, that knowledge was thought to come to us through divine illumination. Yet anyone acquainted with the debates surrounding this doctrine in the Middle Ages knows how elusive the arguments in favor of it can be. This explains in part the enthusiasm generated in the course of the thirteenth century by the recovery of Aristotelian natural philosophy, with all of the new possibilities that it afforded, as

---

38. Augustine, *Soliloquies*, I.2, 7.

well as all of the subtle dangers that it conjured up. For this eventuality Augustine had left his disciples ill prepared. In any case, the rediscovery of an independent realm of nature brought the age of medieval innocence to an abrupt end. The issue was stated most sharply by one of Augustine's disciples, who explicitly equates the tree of the knowledge of good and evil with philosophy and, by implication, the serpent of Genesis with the Aristotelian philosopher.[39] In his desire to achieve the greatest possible clarity about the truth of the Christian faith, Augustine had gone further than any previous Latin writer in attributing to God the ideas that the Bible seems to deny him. The turning point came when it dawned on some of the new Aristotelians that if one already knows what God thinks, one might be spared the necessity of listening to what he has to say.

---

39. St. Bonaventure, Third Sunday of Advent, *Sermon* 2, *Works,* Vol. IX, 62-63. Cf. J. G. Bougerol, *Introduction to the Works of St. Bonaventure* (Patterson, N.J., 1964), 150-51.

Sexuality in Saint Augustine

Robert J. O'Connell, S.J.

There are several strategic decisions to be made at the very outset of any such study as this. Compare the two symposia on this same topic sponsored by the *Journal for the Scientific Study of Religion,* with the more recent study put out by Berkeley's *Center for Hermeneutical Studies,* and you find that both of the former rely heavily on interpretation by means of psychoanalytic models, whereas the latter eschews explicit appeal to all such intermediaries and fastens directly on Augustine's text.[1]

That impression of directness must not, of course, be taken naively: even the most obdurate attempt to bring nothing but plain common sense to bear on interpreting Augustine's psychology will be foiled, so persistent is the swarm of psycho-

---

1. See the issues devoted to Augustine's *Confessions* by the *Journal for the Scientific Study of Religions* (henceforth: *JSSR*), in Vols. 1 and 2 (1965 and 1966), and the studies done more recently, in Vol. 25 (1986), especially: Joseph E. Dittes, "Augustine: Search for a Fail-Safe God to Trust," 57-63; Volney Gay, "Augustine: The Reader as Self-object," 64-76, and Eugene TeSelle, "Augustine as Client and Theorist," 92-101. Compare the article by Peter Brown on "Augustine and Sexuality, " in *Colloquy* 46 (1983), 1-13 (publication of the Center for Hermeneutical Studies, Berkeley, Calif.), along with responses solicited from J. Patout Burns, Xavier Harris, Margaret Miles, and myself (pp. 14-25), and Brown's reply to those responses as well as to other scholars' questions (pp. 28-41). I shall abbreviate references to the above by citing them as Dittes, Gay, and TeSelle (all 1986), and Brown, 1983. (I have added to my original notes, in parentheses, some valuable observations expressed by other participants in this "encounter.")

analytic insights that have become ingredient to our contemporary "common sense." And yet, a commonsensical interpreter like myself cannot but feel that psychoanalytical categories, when applied to Augustine's writings, have proven far from uniformly successful; they often manage to obfuscate, in varying degrees, what they mean to clarify.[2] Besides, the nonprofessional finds it beyond his ken to choose among the rival psychoanalytical models that clamor for application: shall we look for an Oedipal story here, or a pre-Oedipal narcissistic story? Shall we (to mention but several of the candidates different writers have espoused) lean on Freud himself — whether "early" or "late" — or Jung, or Kohut? The layman must admit his incompetence to sort the matter out *except* — except! — in terms of which psychoanalytic model seems to him to illumine Augustine's text without distortion. And by that I mean Augustine's text as a scholar must read it: through the lens of his common sense, but a common sense educated to the man's individual idiom, understood against the background of his century and its culture. Permit this particular layman, then, to trust his educated common sense right from the start, even if it means entrusting the results of his reading, in a next step, to evaluation by professionals of the human psyche.

Even while adopting this "direct" approach to the text, however, we must face a second strategic decision. Shall we take into account that, during his long writing career, Augustine may well have proposed not one, but (in Peter

---

2. Paula Fredriksen, in "Augustine and his Analysts: The Possibility of a Psychohistory," in *Soundings* 61 (1975), 206-27, gives a careful summary and excellent critique of some recent attempts to examine Augustine's sexuality through the lenses of various psychological constructs. She surveys studies by E. R. Dodds and C. Kligerman, plus studies by the authors contributing to Volumes 1 and 2 of *JSSR*, mentioned in note 1, above: D. Bakan, W. H. Clarke, J. Dittes, P. Woolcott, Jr., and P. W. Pruyser, respectively. I shall cite this article as Fredriksen, 1978. While I find the great majority of her critical observations uncannily accurate, I must also suspect, sadly, that in attempting to apply the "narcissistic" construct to Augustine, she herself may have tumbled into more than one fault she finds in others. But I shall spare the reader, for the most part, detailed references to where the reading of Augustine's text I present here clashes with readings given by my predecessors.

Brown's term) two distinct "paradigms" of human sexuality? My enormous respect for Peter Brown is no secret, so it may come as a surprise that I have chosen to table his suggestion, at least for the purposes of this study. Our time is limited, and others besides myself have questioned whether what Brown sees as Augustine's "later" paradigm is really all that distinct from his "earlier" one. (My own restudy of that earlier paradigm has persuaded me that there is more strength in that objection than originally appeared.) But even if Brown's view were entirely correct, he would not deny, I think, that *the* paradigm of sexuality which Augustine bequeathed to history, and which influenced that history in decisive ways, is the "earlier" paradigm. Let us assume, for clarity's sake, that this earlier paradigm runs with fair consistency from the Cassiciacum dialogues up to and through Augustine's *Confessions*. That assumption once made, another reason for tabling Brown's suggestion comes into view: it is plain that the *Confessions*, with or without illumination from those earlier works, embodies the view of sexuality on which the great bulk of previous discussions have focused.

Brown calls Augustine's earlier paradigm "ascetic." Yet even his description of it might be seen to argue for renaming it an "ascetical-mystical" paradigm. "In the air" of late antiquity, it received especially forceful expression from the "radical wing of ascetical Christians," particularly as propounded by Ambrose and his circle. Adam and Eve were created by God to be, and to remain, asexual beings, in "angelic" bodies "untouched by sexuality," all their bliss deriving from their "'angelic' contemplation of God." From this state they "fell" into the "present 'material' mode of being," into the sexual differentiation and "'cares of this world'" familiar to us all. Hence withdrawal from human society to embrace the ascetical (and, I would add, contemplative) life was looked on as a partial return to the angelic joys of Adam's and Eve's prelapsarian state.[3]

Brown's picture seems to me thus far unexceptionable. The same is true, for the most part, of his summary of

---

3. Brown, 1983, 5-6.

Augustine's life experience — including that of sex — which largely accounted for the attraction this paradigm held for the convert of A.D. 386. All too regularly, though, this is precisely the stage at which writers on this topic begin to justify their divergent views of Augustine's sexuality, so a brief review of that life experience is in order.

The literature on this topic boils over with talk of the "terrible strength" of Augustine's sexual passions, of this "ex-profligate" bishop who became the "fountainhead of that pruriency" which has since defiled Western theology.[4] Elaine Pagels only adds the newest installment: Augustine's later attitudes stem from the "insatiable" violence of his lusts, for he was "a man who never married [sic] and whose experience of sexual pleasure was illicit and guilt-provoking."[5] Yet compare such statements with O'Meara's depiction of Augustine's premarital exploits as no more than average for the Carthage of his time,[6] and Peter Brown's estimate that his perfectly respectable relationship (best called a "common-law marriage") with the mother of his son provided "nine years of unproblematic enjoyment of sexual companionship,"[7] and there is obviously a conflict of interpretations here. What was Augustine's sexual experience like, and how did it affect his later attitudes and teaching on sexuality?

Our best procedure will be follow the story as told in the *Confessions;* not only is it our richest single source, but (as we observed earlier) it has invariably been the primary focus for the discussions of Augustine's sexuality. The moment we get past the Proemium (I, 1-6), we are plunged into a description of early infancy dominated by images of maternal breasts.[8]

---

4. Quoted by Brown, ibid., 1.

5. See Elaine Pagels, *Adam, Eve, and the Serpent* (New York, 1988), 141; see also 105 (cited henceforth as Pagels, 1988). (Ernest Fortin reminded me in this connection of how difficult it is to identify Augustine's "dominant passion," and how dangerous it would be to oversimplify his psychological makeup.)

6. See John J. O'Meara, *The Young Augustine* (London, 1954), 47-52 (henceforth: *Young Augustine*).

7. Brown, 1983, 3.

8. As Gay, 1986, 71, 75, rightly stresses.

Soon we are told that the milk which nourished the infant
Augustine came, not "from" but "through" those human
breasts, from God himself: or, is it "herself"? Here, as so often
throughout the *Confessions* (and his preached works also),
Augustine images God as a nursing, consoling, tenderly caring
mother. He had, to be sure, plenty of biblical encouragement
for this imagery (and for the affect accompanying it); Isaiah
alone provided a wealth of inspiration on which he clearly
drew.[9] But many another preacher and writer had been exposed
to the same Isaian imagery without being inspired to create the
symphony on God's maternal "care" which the *Confessions* represents. Here, as in all such cases of "selective influence," we
are thrown back upon the predispositions the influenced
author brings to his reading, as well as to his other fonts of
imaginative experience.

Before we conclude, however, that Augustine's was the
ideal God for Monica's "momma's boy,"[10] we must take into
account that a number of his feminine God-images are more
"spousal" than maternal in character,[11] and that on this score
also he received considerable encouragement, from pagan as
well as from biblical literature.

Finally, it must be acknowledged that Augustine's
"masculine" images of God are (at first blush, anyway) much
sterner in character: they regularly have to do with judgment,
chastisement, healing, and curing by means of burning, cutting,
and so forth. One might be tempted to argue that these masculine images support Dittes's claim that Augustine's God is "re-
mote,"[12] but even that claim is partial at best, and how Dittes

---

9. For documentation, see my articles, "The God of St. Augustine's
Imagination" and "Isaiah's Mothering God in St. Augustine's *Confessions*,"
both in *Thought*, the former in 57 (1982), 30-40; the latter in 58 (1983),
188-206. Also: *Imagination and Metaphysics in St. Augustine* (Milwaukee,
1987) (Annual Aquinas Lecture).

10. Dittes, 1986, 138.

11. See Paul Rigby, "Paul Ricoeur, Freudianism, and Augus-
tine's *Confessions*," in *Journal of the American Academy of Religion* 53 (1985),
93-114, p. 108n.1. See also the comment on pp. 115-27 of the same issue by
Donald Capps, "Augustine as Narcissist." (I shall cite these as Rigby, 1985
and Capps, 1985.)

12. Dittes, 1986, 61-62. (William Babcock wisely advised against

can have missed the closeness and the caring tenderness of the maternal (to say nothing of the spousal) God is simply beyond me. It is also worth observing that it is the maternal God whom Augustine regularly depicts in those marvelous paradoxes of omnipresence, which manifest his keen awareness that the "nearness" of God's presence is not opposed to, but actually requires, the "remoteness" of genuine transcendence. Similarly, he seems convinced that God must possess masculine as well as feminine traits if he/she is to exist "beyond" the limitations of either. The more remarkable thing, though, is the sensitivity with which he depicts God's feminine side, and, as we shall have occasion to see, the boldness of the frankly sexual imagery he brings to that depiction.

For the moment, then, suffice it to warn the reader that Augustine will view the "conversion" to God which he relates in his *Confessions* as quite literally a "return": of the prodigal to his Father; of a straying child to his mother; of an Odysseus to Penelope, his bride. This immediately suggests, of course, that there may have been some original "aversion" and "straying away" from that same God, but this need not directly concern us now.

Augustine now dwells on how he imagines an infant learns the rudiments of speech. We need not agree with his psychology either of infancy or of language to inquire what his point is. I suggest that he is driving at "exercising the mind" of his reader — a favorite teaching technique of his — to provoke the realization that our life of consciousness and volition is conducted "inside" the opaque "vestment" or "dwelling" of the body. We cannot communicate directly with the "interior" of another; we must resort to all the roundabout techniques of symbolic expression, thus learning the painful lesson that we can never adequately communicate the richness of our spiritual

granting Dittes too much on this point: even the initial "remoteness" of Augustine's masculine God-images quickly yields to the intimacies of God as *susceptor,* "taking us up" reassuringly as a father, doctor, or lawyer would an adopted child or a trusting client. At the same time, Ernest Fortin observed how frequently Augustine, in his early works especially, dwells on the motif of "fear," and particularly on the fear of death; is this because death might come as an appropriate punishment? The theme would be worth researching.)

lives by means of those blunt bodily instrumentalities. As a Platonist, Augustine is convinced that the "inner word" is always superior, and the "outer word" (however eloquent or artistically accomplished it may *seem*) is always a comedown, a traitorous translation at best, of the inner word it is meant to suggest to another's interior.

Strictly speaking, the image of the soul-body relationship Augustine is working with here violates the canons of his theory. To follow TeSelle's reminder[13] of Newman's famous distinction, the "notional" theory laid down in the *De Quantitate Animae* would suggest that the soul not be thought of as "in" the body. But this is not the only instance where the "notional," for Augustine, fails to rhyme with how he "really" thinks. Pay close attention to the images which are actually operative when he speaks of the body as *vestimentum, habitus, habitaculum*, or even *habitatio*, and you will find that the "mortal body" we bear about us in "this" lower world "surrounds" the soul very like an opaque cloak or housing; it makes it impossible for one "interior" to intuit another directly, and consequently makes it possible for us to dissimulate and lie to one another. This hiatus between mind-soul and mortal body makes Augustine suspicious of all avenues of symbolic communication: it would never spontaneously occur to him, for instance, to think of sexual activity as a form of authentically human "conversation," a way (much less the completest human way) in which spouses could express their tenderness and love for one another.

In another image for this relationship, drawn from his early works (*Mus.*, VI, 13-14) and incorporated into his *Confessions*, he pictures the soul as ideally situated "above," and therefore governing the body which is "subordinate" to it. But humanity's sinful condition has turned that order upside down, so that the rebellious body strives to govern the soul. Augustine comes to think of the human genitals as the primary locus of that unruliness which dislocates, and sets the mortal body into rebellious disrelation with the "I" which he identifies as mind-soul. Once we attempt to play the game of mutual love in sexual terms, he is persuaded, we inevitably get swept away

13. TeSelle, 1986, 96.

into another game entirely — the game of lustful exploitation which the mortal body stubbornly insists on playing.

In dealing with this topic, it should not be forgotten that we have to do with a North African temperament: we cannot know for sure the exact blood-mix Augustine derived from his parents, but the resulting solution was almost certainly, as Mandouze puts it, "hot, impulsive, and given to extremes."[14] This seems to have been Monica's judgment, and her principal reason for delaying her son's baptism. Augustine speculates that she deemed that the guilt *(reatus)* of sins committed after baptism would be "greater and more dangerous" (I, 17) than those committed by a catechumen who remained unbaptized. The penitential practice of the ancient church may also have been a factor: for several centuries the sin of adultery (along with murder and apostasy), when committed by a baptized person, required the austere regime of public penitence for its remission, whereas adult baptism was thought to cleanse the soul at a stroke. How was the young Augustine expected to respond to this half-fatalistic attitude? Did he even notice?

Augustine assures us that he did. As a child, he became dangerously ill and, while hovering close to death, he begged and pleaded for baptism. His mother was on the point of giving in, when suddenly he took a turn for the better and the baptismal plans were put on "hold" once again. The memory is evidently a vivid one, and Augustine intimates the message this tactic sent to him: that Monica regarded it as "quasi-necessary that [he] would be stained" by sins as he grew older (I, 17)! The saying was a common one, Augustine assures us: "Let him be, let him do it; for he is not yet baptized!" And Monica knew well "what mighty storms of temptations" would menace her son during adolescence (I, 18).

Monica exhibits a similar laissez-faire attitude on the occasion when Patricius detects that his son has become "vested in [a body of] restless adolescence," and exultantly brings the glad news home. Augustine's report is highly suggestive:

---

14. See André Mandouze, *Saint Augustine: L'Aventure de la Raison et de la Grâce* (Paris, 1968), 74. Mandouze, be it noted, has lived much of his life in North Africa.

though his father was only a catechumen, God "had already *begun*" *(iam inchoaveras)* to make Monica his temple. So, despite the fact that her son was "not yet one of the faithful" *(nondum fideli)*, she admonished him "secretly" and "with immense solicitude, that [he] not fornicate, and most important of all *(maximeque)*, that [he] not commit adultery with anyone's wife" (II, 6-7). Surely this sounds very like the cynical old saw, "if you can't be good, be careful"; it would scarcely put needed spine into a hot-blooded sixteen-year-old's resolve to remain chaste.

The very next paragraph (II, 8) underlines the same estimate of Monica. Augustine complains that despite her acknowledgment of the dangers surrounding him, her recommendations of chastity went entirely unsupported by any practical moves, like arranging a marriage for her son. And the reasoning he attributes to her *(ita enim conicio recolens)* shows why he pictures her as having fled "the very center of Babylon" but as "loitering still in its outskirts." It had nothing to do with hopes for the next life; she feared that a wife would prove an obstacle to the this-worldly hopes that she, as well as Patricius, were pinning on their brilliant son's success in his studies! Soon afterward, Augustine is sent (without, apparently, any thought of supervision) to pursue those studies in Madaura, and subsequently in Carthage, a city notorious at that epoch for the opportunities it afforded for every form of vice.

Years later, when Augustine's Milanese conversion approaches, Monica's attitude and tactics remain much the same: Augustine awakens one day to find that his common-law wife has been sent home to Africa, evidently as part of a deal which will assure Milan's municipal *rhetor* of the high-society marriage which will further his brilliant career. Once enclosed in that final corral of safety, though, Augustine can also seriously think of baptism; all in good time! But it can scarcely be contended that, until this arrangement for her son's worldly future had been nailed down, either baptism or chastity ranked high among Monica's effective priorities. Augustine takes an interim mistress: there is not a whisper about a complaint from Monica. Her devotion to Augustine had much of the "daughter of Eve" about it (V, 15), and the message was not lost on her son.

Yet why put the burden entirely on Monica — what of Patricius's influence on his son? Ah, dear old Patricius, what a "bum rap" he has been given; first by his son, then by interpreters of his son's *Confessions*. What do we really know of him? We have just considered his reaction to seeing his son in the baths (which, I protest, hardly merits Dittes's rancid label, a "bawdy locker room initiation").[15] We have also seen that Patricius agreed with Monica about giving their son the best education possible, and (even Augustine seems impressed by this!) went well beyond his means, indeed, went temporarily broke, in his efforts to finance that education. That much, plus Augustine's depiction of his parents' relationship in Book IX, and our impressions of Patricius have very little to go on. We have even less to go on, incidentally, in the case of Augustine's siblings!

But Monica, her son tells us in Book IX, "endured [Patricius's] injurious treatment in her marriage bed" without making any great fuss about it (IX, 19). Yet in saying *toleravit cubilis iniurias,* does the Bishop really mean (as translators and interpreters seem unquestioningly to have assumed) that Patricius was "unfaithful" (Pagels inflates this to "habitually unfaithful") to his wife? And was the boy Augustine aware of this? If so, Patricius, too, must be held guilty of undercutting his son's resolve in his adolescent sexual battles. In that case, though, we would expect an angry Augustine to limn his father in tones far less pale than those he uses. The tones he applies appear (to me, at least) too washed out to suggest that Patricius was emotionally important to his son, much less that he was in any credible sense the object of Augustine's "Oedipal rage." Augustine tells us, in a chilling sentence, that Monica strove determinedly to make God, not Patricius, Augustine's true "father" (I, 17). She seems to have succeeded only too well: when Patricius dies, it takes Augustine several paragraphs of narration to catch up and remind his readers of the fact.

Let me conclude with my own suspicion: that the "injurious treatment" Monica had to suffer from her husband may well have been prompted by his excess of human affection for

---

15. Dittes, 1986, 61.

her, an excess which inflamed him to require his *droit de mari* with a frequency, or on occasions, which his (quite possibly) puritanically righteous wife considered unseemly. It would not surprise me if the Bishop of Hippo, who urged abstention from marital relations during Lent (*Sermones* 207, 208, 209), preached that marital intercourse was venially sinful unless for purposes of procreation (*Sermo* 51, 21-22), and could mock Julian of Eclanum so bitingly about his rosier view of sexuality,[16] would take (or even conjecturally invent for us) his mother's censorious view of the matter. In any event, it would be extremely chancy to employ this assumption about Patricius's alleged "infidelity" to ground any conclusions concerning Augustine's sexual attitudes.

Nevertheless it is time to say a word or two about Augustine's rhetoric of sinfulness.[17] For it would be lethal to bring a naively literal mind to interpreting certain of his expressions. Throughout Book I, for example, he is portraying his infancy (I, 7-12) and childhood (*pueritia:* I, 13-31). Only at II, 1 does he begin his lurid description of the adolescence he dates from his sixteenth year. At I, 16 he lists the sins of his *pueritia,* and it is worth noting that while two of Augustine's classic triad, pride and curiosity, receive mention, significantly concupiscence of the flesh goes unmentioned. Its time is not yet come. Yet it would seem that he cannot resist the (apparently)

---

16. See *Contra Julianum,* III, 28, especially in what Fredriksen (1978, 226n.26) rightly terms the "energetic translation" found in Peter Brown's *Augustine of Hippo* (Berkeley, 1967), 391. (Both Karen Jo Torjesen and Jean Bethke Elshtain expressed their reserves on the possible anachronism they detected in my depiction of Patricius: the pagan marriage mores of the time would have sanctioned his expending his sexual energies on slave girls and/or concubines: no need for him to be a nuisance to Monica. But is it entirely too innocent to imagine that Patricius may have just plain loved his wife more than such [twentieth-century?] promiscuity would imply? Augustine's elaborate expression in *Confessions,* IX, 19 is striking: Monica's comportment made her *pulchram . . . et reverenter amabilem atque mirabilem viro [suo].* In any case, I would still hold to my main conclusion: we cannot be sure that Augustine is telling us Patricius was unfaithful, and so would be ill-advised to draw any inferences from that assumption.)

17. Compare my observations here with those of O'Meara, in *Young Augustine,* 8-9.

hyperbolic trope, *tantillus puer et tantus peccator,* even when the "sin" was not liking school, and his elders' ignoble hopes in sending him there aimed at his later being able to "satiate the insatiable lusts after plenteous want and ignominious glory" (*satiandas insatiabiles cupiditates copiosae inopiae et ignominiosae gloriae:* I, 19). Tough language, but observe that the two "lusts" are directed at riches and glory, respectively, not sexual pleasure; yet they are both "insatiable," for (Augustine the Platonist knows) *cupiditas* is by its very nature insatiable![18]

But sex makes a deceptive entrance when the boy Augustine is put to studying literature. He will try, in an afterthought, partially to exculpate his mother by speculating that she hoped the normal course of studies would be "no obstacle, but even some help to [her son] toward attaining [God]" (II, 8); but now he protests (applying his *uti-frui* distinction) that his more elementary studies in reading, writing, and calculating have proven far more "useful" to him; indeed, the "delight" (I, 26: *delectabar*) he took in reading about the love affairs of Dido, Aeneas, and Jupiter (I, 20-26) amounted to a species of "fornication against [God]" (I, 21). He goes on to explain, however, that sex is not the issue here; he means by "fornication" the preferential love of "*this* world" which, 1 John 2:15-16 warns us, can take the triadic form of pride, fleshly concupiscence, and curiosity. "I forsook You, and went in pursuit of the lowermost of Your creatures, I who was earth, going toward earth." That, I suggest, is Augustine's image for the primal "iniquity" (VII, 22) which, precisely as in Peter Brown's "ascetic paradigm," plunged our "weighted" souls downward from the heights of angelic bliss to the restless pursuit of lowermost "earthly" and temporal delights. This, I also suggest, is the pretemporal act of archetypal "fornication" which accounted for our souls' original "fall"; but the dynamism of that fall continues to work through infant, child, and adolescent, unmasking even a "little lad" as quite literally a "great sinner": *tantillus puer et tantus peccator.*

I submit that what sometimes seems like overblown rhetoric may spring from a deeper stratum of meaning which trans-

---

18. A point that escapes Pagels, 1988, 105.

mutes apparent hyperboles into dark ironies. Even childhood peccadilloes are surface revelations of a sinful dynamic whose venom wells up from an act performed in the unconstrained plenitude of angelic freedom. The plenitude of that freedom has been lost to us in consequence (see *De Libero Arbitrio*, III, 34-35), yet even the acts we now commit out of moral "ignorance and difficulty" can disclose a gravity and poignancy which fully justifies (to Augustine's eyes) what we could mistakenly read as rhetorical overkill. For if his theory be credited, every sin we commit, including that of bodily fornication, is a renewed instance of our primordial "turning away" to love "this world" in preference to God, and a fresh ratification of our soul's original "fornication" from him.

Sexuality in the proper sense of the term comes massively on the scene with Augustine's sixteenth year, his entry on adolescence. *Confessions*, II, 1 opens with a barrage of near-Swiftian imagery: filth, corruption, fevers, and the stench and stain of rank jungle growth. Students of Augustine's prose and historical period have rightly expressed impatience with those who interpret his "varied and shadowy loves" as pointing toward homosexual adventures.[19] But he is scarcely easy on himself: like so many romantics before and after him, he was in love with love, but so blinded (he tells us) by the mists of carnal desire that he could not distinguish between the brightness of friendship and the murkiness of bodily lust. Like the prodigal son, he kept going even further away from his divine Father, while (simultaneously!) like Odysseus he was "tossed about and spilt forth" into the stormy seas of passion. Suddenly that metaphor of fluidity takes a frankly biological turn: his "fornications made him boil over and flow outward in all directions." The result: he is overcome by a "restless weariness," *inquieta lassitudine* (II, 2).

That phrase is a near-perfect match for the one Augustine uses later: artists who observe no norm for the "use" of their beautiful productions only "wander farther away" from God

---

19. Fredriksen, 1978, p. 210 (cf. p. 207), cites Bonner and Marrou as students of Augustine who were "annoyed" (and justly so) by such wildly suspicious readings of Augustine's text.

and "spew forth their strength into weary languors": *in deliciosas lassitudines* (X, 53). In fact, the later passage helps interpret the earlier. Augustine is picturing himself (here as so often elsewhere: see I, 28) as a composite of prodigal and Odysseus: both were ancient world metaphors for the soul that wandered away and eventually returned home. Both of them encountered sensual temptations, the prodigal among harlots, Odysseus on Circe's island, but among the lotus eaters as well. The danger for both of them was to "forget" they were on a homeward journey and to tarry, regarding the beauties surrounding them not as objects of "use," temporary respites to help them voyage further, but literally as "stopping places," objects of terminal "delight" and "enjoyment": *frui.* That precise form of "lust" *(cupiditas)* which is sexual, Augustine is saying here, seduced him into regarding the human beauties he encountered as objects of just such terminal "enjoyment." Having "spewed forth" the strength he should have conserved for journeying back to God, he then experienced the post-coital "weariness" that can be both sweet and languorous, and at the same time "restless" on account of the nagging sense of duty deferred.

But there is a hidden irony here: Augustine's scheme implies that had he loved his partners-in-lust with the more spiritual love of "friendship" *(amicitia),* he would have loved them not with the love of "enjoyment" but with the more appropriate love of "use." This has been pointed out, in tones of disappointment, by a number of writers,[20] and I find myself entirely in sympathy with them. Augustine has adopted (and all too inflexibly, alas) an over-simple set of categories for thinking out the various forms of love, and when it comes to situating our love for human beings, those categories leave him no other option. True, there is that hybrid form he proposes in *De Trinitate,* XI, 10, *frui in via:* we may enjoy other persons in somewhat the way we enjoy the lovely appointments of a traveler's inn. But since we should enjoy neither in such a way as to allow them to detain us from our homeward journey, this is patently a form of *uti* rather than of *frui,* when all is said.

---

20. See Capps, 1985, 126-27; Fredriksen, 1978, 222-23; and in partial defense of Augustine, TeSelle, 1986, 99.

I began by saying that there was a hidden irony running through Augustine's thinking on lust *versus* friendship. The irony is this: he will quite soon tell us of his first literary product, a little work on aesthetics called *De Pulchro et Apto* (IV, 20ff.). The title itself implies the basic distinction on which the work is built, that there are certain types of good in the sense that they are *aptum*, befitting in the sense of benefiting some other being: a shoe that is "good" in this sense, Augustine would have us consider *aptum*. But, Augustine continues, there is another type of being which "is a whole, as it were, and therefore beautiful." Such things, he clearly means, are good in and of themselves, without our having to ground their goodness — or better, their "beauty" — on their relationship of being "good *for*" some other being which they benefit or "befit."

Here, I submit, we see Augustine lucidly pointing to a property which "beauty" shares with the ideal sort of "friend" (in Aristotle's theory, surely familiar to Augustine from Cicero's *De Amicitia*). Both exhibit a type of excellence which invites, even compels us, temporarily to suspend all traces of self-interest and self-concern, all "narcissistic" considerations if you will, and simply lose ourselves in admiring the excellence of the friend, or the beauty of the aesthetic phenomenon before us. This, I take it, is the attitude narcissism theory refers to as genuine "object-love." O'Donovan[21] classifies it as "rational love," though I question whether he does justice to how regularly Augustine appeals to it precisely in an aesthetic context. But trace the fortunes of his aesthetic thinking and, I suggest, you will find that each time this "object-love" attitude comes into conflict (even if only half-acknowledged conflict) with Augustine's "order of goods," the terminal quality of unselfconcerned "object-love" regularly disappears, its *frui* character increasingly boiled down to a form of *uti*.[22] And that reduction-

---

21. TeSelle's "partial defense" (note 20, above) refers to Oliver O'Donovan's work, *The Problem of Self-Love in St. Augustine* (New Haven, 1980), 29-32.

22. See my *Art and the Christian Intelligence in St. Augustine* (Cambridge, Mass., 1978), 137-40.

ism is exactly what is at work in the passages we have just been considering. The reduction can occur very swiftly: here we see it working in the very same book of the *Confessions* which contains the aesthetic insight which should have obviated it; it occurs, in fact, in the very paragraphs which precede (IV, 14-15) and which follow (IV, 30) expression of that insight. One can only conclude that Augustine's appreciation of "object-love" was unsteady at best, far too weak to stand up against the momentum of his *uti-frui* distinction.

Yet TeSelle's wise caution again comes to mind: the *uti-frui* distinction could well have worked more in the "notional" order than in the order of Augustine's "real" assents. There is something abstract and bloodless about that distinction, and we are talking here about a full-blooded individual who had, from all accounts, a positive "genius for friendship." Does not the evidence tell us that he "lived" his friendships far more faithfully, even passionately, than this chill theory would sanction?[23] One could argue further that the mental gymnastics to which Augustine puts himself in *De Trinitate* clearly point to his serious discomfort with this distinction. Didn't he, at least as intelligent as we moderns, keenly *feel* the inadequacy of this conceptual straitjacket, even though his mind was insufficiently stocked with alternative categories for dealing with the problem?

On the other hand, we must also allow for that power human consciousness unquestionably has, of "creating" modes and limits of feeling and evaluating which, over time, can inhibit, recast, even "falsify" our saner, more spontaneous, and "natural" ways of feeling. Every physician knows that a psychosomatic headache hurts just as much as a "real" one, just as every therapist must deal with patients who have come "really" to live in the world their neurotic fantasies have constructed about them. So also (to anticipate on another issue), we must not allow our own conviction that Manichaeism is a farrago of nonsense to prevent us from acknowledging that over a good span of years Augustine's world, both inner and outer, "*was* that way" for *him*.

23. See TeSelle, 1986, 94-95.

How, though, shall we decide what friendship love really, not only notionally, "was for him"? My preferred solution comes from probing beneath the conceptual surface into the world of Augustine's lively imagination. Concepts may counterfeit, but our imaginations betray what reality genuinely "is" for each of us. And I have found Augustine, especially in his preached works, repeatedly duplicating the performance which launched us into this particular meditation. Subtending the *uti-frui* framework, and infusing it with the heat of passion, you will regularly detect the pulse beat of the image which sums up for him, more than any other, his feeling for our human situation: *peregrinatio*. Like the prodigal, we are wayfarers; like the Israelites, wanderers in a desert; like Odysseus, voyagers. Our greatest tragedy, our heartbreaking failure would be to get so comfortable with the amenities of our journeying as never to "arrive" back at our Father's "house"; back to the breasts of the "Heavenly Jerusalem, our Mother"; back to the spousal embrace of Penelope, ancient figure of Wisdom, whom we long ago left behind, but never completely forgot. Strangeness, alienation; insecurity and danger; hunger, thirst, and insatiable longing; "restlessness": these are the feelings Augustine entertained for "this" twilight world, this "region of unlikeness"; entertained and deliberately cultivated, and strove tirelessly to make his flock entertain them as well.

Yet notice once again that what draws us upward and away from bodily sex is this spiritual "appetite" for "beatitude": beatitude which is only the more attractive for embodying, on a higher, spiritual level, all the allure of sexual union. This is the aspect which persuades me to call Augustine's earlier sexual paradigm not simply "ascetic, " but "ascetical-mystical."

This same affective tonality and image-complex make a powerful reappearance in the *Hortensius* episode which writers habitually, and correctly, refer to as Augustine's "first conversion." Augustine describes his coming to Carthage, that "cauldron of shameful loves" and, still "in love with love," he seems to have known more than one sexual adventure before having "gained love's bond of joy" in a union that also taught him "jealousy, suspicion, anger and fear, and quarreling" (III, 1). We shall take a closer look at that union in a moment.

About this same time, however, when he was nineteen years of age, he happened on the text of Cicero's "exhortation to philosophy," his call for his readers to abandon the life of worldly action in order to adopt the near-monkish simplicity and contemplative detachment of the "philosophical" mode of life. There is no reason to think Augustine exaggerated the effect of this reading, for the *Hortensius* incident is repeatedly and enthusiastically recalled in the Cassiciacum dialogues as well as in his later works. But it is important to notice the frankly erotic imagery he uses to describe the attractions of the contemplative life. With "incredible ardor of heart [he] longed after the immortality of Wisdom," a Wisdom of manifestly feminine character. "How I burned, my God, how I burned to fly back from earthly realities to You . . . for with You is Wisdom": *apud Te est Sapientia*, as St. John's Prologue tells us. *Surgere coeperam ut ad Te redirem:* he had already "begun to rise up," like the prodigal, "in order to return" from harlots to Wisdom's chaste embraces. (The expected paternal image is notably absent!) Lest we fail to notice these overtones of passion, he insists: "I was stirred up, and enkindled, and set aflame, to love, and seek after, pursue and catch hold of, and strongly embrace . . . Wisdom Herself" (III, 8). That same erotic imagery will return when Book VIII portrays Augustine's nostalgic recall of the *Hortensius,* just as he is about to surrender, finally, to the attractions of the contemplative life.

Now Augustine tells us of his conversion to Manichaeism. His first move after reading the *Hortensius* was to take up the Gospels; he found their style too lowly for his taste. But we know from his other writings that he also encountered problems with reconciling the divergent genealogies of Christ in Matthew and Luke, and that the Manichees confronted him with a host of similar "intellectual" problems with Catholicism's Scriptures and doctrine. In short, Augustine's primary motive for becoming a Manichee does appear to have been intellectual in nature. This does not mean that it was anything less than a sincerely "religious" conversion: the beloved name of Christ, which he could not find in the *Hortensius,* was forever on the Manichees' lips. They were, to his young eyes, more "intellectual" Christians than the Catholics. It is a mistake,

therefore, and one frequently made, to think that Augustine
meant us to regard his Milanese "conversion" as a passage from
"paganism" to Christianity.

But the "otherworldly" message of the *Hortensius*, coming
to one whose adolescent sexuality seems to have found a quiet
haven in marriage, may have lent added attractiveness to the
Manichees' claims to a loftier "purity" than Catholics possessed.
In any event, the recent convert would soon have been introduced to that Manichee pretension, and, knowing Augustine's
style, it was likely to cast a certain spell upon him. So, we shall
have to remain alert to the possibility that Manichee "purity"
could have complexified Augustine's longish experience of
married sex.

For the moment, though, this much should be clear: the
most accurate term we can apply to the union Augustine entered
at this time is "marriage." The woman was evidently a com-
moner, and would have expected (from a brilliant "comer" like
Augustine) no more than a "second-class marriage." But theirs
was a perfectly respectable union, in the eyes of both state and
church, and Augustine states roundly that he was "faithful" to
her for the dozen or so years they lived together. Monica, who
objected so strongly to living under the same roof with her son
when he became a Manichee, apparently raised no objections
whatever to living with her daughter-in-law. Hence Brown's
conjecture that Augustine's sexual experience during that considerable period would have been "unproblematic."[24]

We shall see, in time, persuasive grounds for agreeing
substantially with Brown's judgment, but it must be admitted
that there are also, for the moment at least, reasons for questioning it. Grant, for a moment, that Augustine would have reso-
nated with the Manichee pretensions toward the higher purity;
now take account of their teaching on sexuality. Our souls, they
taught, are all sparks of the Divine Light, imprisoned in the Evil
principle, filthy Matter. The greatest sin a Manichee could commit was that of procreating: for this only imprisoned the divinity for at least another generation. The "auditors" or rank-and-
file Manichees could marry, and even engage in sexual

---

24. Brown, 1983, 2-3.

intercourse; such activity, they were assured, was the doing of their bodies, hence of the evil Matter which was opposed to their real selves. They were expected, however, to take careful steps to assure that procreation did not occur, and the Manichee devices on this score, including surprisingly detailed instructions about calculating the woman's "safe period," must have induced a measure of anxiety. What a breeding ground of guilt complexes: while procreation was the greatest of sins, sexual intercourse, in and of itself, had no moral qualification whatever — it was neither good nor bad!

And yet, to further complicate matters, the Manichees of the sect's inner circle, the "elect," were required to live in unsullied celibacy. And they alone could hope, at death, to escape the imprisonment of Matter and be reunited with the Divine Light. There was a gaping inconsistency here, one which Augustine must have felt keenly even if he failed to conceptualize it clearly. There must be something reprehensible about sexual activity, after all, if it could prevent a serious aspirant from attaining to "first-class citizenship" in the Manichee world: and one suspects that an Augustine did not settle very contentedly for second class.

Add to all this the devastating fact that, very early in their marriage, the couple actually had a child — and one they named, paradoxically, Adeodatus: "Gift from God." What did Augustine intend by choosing that name? It was, we are told, the Latin form of a common Punic name; and yet no one was ever more sensitive than Augustine to the meanings of words, and the implications of names. Moreover, Augustine speaks with awe of his son's exceptional talents. Was there a hint of defiance here, a profession that despite what Manichee teaching might claim, this child was, indeed, a gift of God?

However one chooses to answer those questions, this much is clear: there may have been turbulent aspects to being a young Manichee auditor named Augustine, living in a common-law marriage which has already produced an outstandingly gifted boy. Would all this have made for an entirely "unproblematic" experience of sex? We cannot decide that issue *a priori:* it will be best to wait on further evidence.

Pierre Courcelle once suggested that Augustine's marital

fidelity proved that Manichee morality on this score must have been fairly exigent. H. I. Marrou replied to that conjecture by asking: "Dare I pronounce, in a stage whisper, the word 'love'?" But despite my admiration for the finesse of that rejoinder, I must confess that I find Augustine's inability to pronounce that word in this connection profoundly unsettling. The complaint that he never gives us his companion's name can cut more ways than one: he never gives the name of the dear friend whose death, described in Book IV of the *Confessions*, came close to breaking his young heart. But despite romanticized translations to the contrary, his exact words describing the effect of his wife's departure back to Africa are scarcely reassuring: she was "torn from his side" *(avulsa a latere meo)* as an "obstacle" to the marriage being planned for him — by Monica, plainly. In consequence, his "heart, to which she adhered, was torn and wounded, and left a trail of blood." Did Augustine intend this language to say he "loved her," as we moderns would mean that phrase?

If so, he certainly chose an ambiguous manner of saying it. *Ubi adhaerebat:* we can say we are "deeply attached" to someone without adverting to the origin of that image.[25] But examine Augustine's usage, and he is quite consistent: he applies the various forms of *haerere* to convey the literally "adhesive" property, the characteristic whereby the lover and the object of his love "stick to," become "nailed" or "glued" to one another.

The usage is traditionally Platonic, and is often fraught — as here, I suggest — with pejorative associations: such loves, when "earthly," make their lovers as earthly as themselves, and consequently "weigh" them down; so, in one of Augustine's favorite texts, the "corruptible body weighs down the soul: *adgravat animam* (Wis. 9:15). But in the spiritual sphere, that

---

25. Notice the translation ("deeply attached") on which Dittes relies, 1986, 60. (Fr. Gerald Ettlinger, S.J., who was kind enough to read this essay, has inquired if Augustine may not also have associated the term *adhaerere* with Genesis 2:24, where the Vulgate uses that Latinism for man's "clinging" to his wife. The question could be worth pursuing, but the curious fact is that the text Augustine used for his earliest exegesis of Genesis [*Contra Manichaeos*, II, 1] read *adjungetur,* whereas later, the text underlying *De Genesi ad litteram* [IX, 1] read *conglutinabitur.*)

transformative property of love permits Augustine's imagination to leap from beholding, to embracing, to becoming literally "one" with the beloved: as John's First Epistle (3:2) tells us (another favorite text), we shall be "like" God — eternal by sharing in his own eternity — because we shall "see him as he [unchangingly, eternally] is." Only the spiritual love of the contemplative, Augustine is intimating, climaxes in the perfect unity of lover and beloved which is feebly foreshadowed in the act of physical intercourse.

Book VIII of the *Confessions* brings home the important point that his "conversion" was not a break from sexual attachments alone, but also from the "worldly hopes" for secular success which, he told us earlier, had lost much (not all!) of their hold over him when he read the *Hortensius*. But we shall discover that Augustine images the break from sexual attachments in a fashion consistent with everything we have seen thus far.

His purpose in consulting the old priest Simplicianus was precisely to get clear on whether he, Augustine, disposed precisely as *he* was *(sic affecto ut ego eram)*, should now live married or celibate (VIII, 1-2). For Paul's words to the Corinthians had made it clear to him that marriage was a perfectly acceptable alternative for Catholics as such. We would be mistaken, therefore, to read the eighth book of the *Confessions* as though Augustine were recounting his conversion to the Catholica; he considers himself already a Catholic, even though a Catholic catechumen. But we would be equally mistaken in supposing that he ever envisaged his own conversion to celibacy as a mandatory model for other Catholics.

Simplicianus's account of Victorinus's conversion prompts him to pray in erotic terms strongly reminiscent of the *Hortensius* episode: "Waken us, [Lord], and call us back; enflame us, and bear us away; make us ardent and draw us by Your sweetness; let us love You, and run to You" (VIII, 9). But, he tells us, "I was sweetly weighed down by the burden of this world, just as often occurs in sleep . . . when a torpid heaviness pervades every limb." This is the same (quite possibly post-coital) *inquieta lassitudo* we saw earlier, to which the sleeper "yields the more gladly, even though [now] it displeases him to do so, since the time for rising draws near" (VIII, 12). Ponti-

cianus visits him, and rambles on about St. Antony's conversion to the desert life, about the monasteries of contemplatives
on the very outskirts of Milan, and about the conversion of
three of his fellow "agents" to the contemplative life (VIII,
13-15). This brings flooding back the memory of Cicero's
Hortensius, and how it had "aroused [him] to the pursuit of
Wisdom" (VIII, 17). He feels himself "held down" by the chain
of sinful habit, by attachment to his "loves of old."

At this point Augustine conducts us through that unfor-
gettable drama of the human will, "wounded" *(semisaucia)* as
punishment for that "freer sin" committed "in Adam" (VIII,
22), and bound by the cumulative cords of subsequently
formed sinful "habit." He finds himself impotent to "will firmly
and finally" to adopt the new form of life which beckons to him
(VIII, 10-12, 19-27).

All his efforts to will that change prove futile. Then, a
vision suddenly dawns upon him; his description of it is shot
through with paradoxes. But it is, typically, the vision of a
feminine figure whose beauty attracts him with the *delectatio
victrix* which Augustine identifies with the "drawing" action of
divine grace. He beholds "the chaste dignity of Continence";
regal and maternal at first impression, in the next instant she
is youthfully "serene and joyous, yet nowise lasciviously so."
She is "alluring" as any courtesan could be, but at the same
time "virtuously alluring," beckoning him to "come to her, and
hesitate no longer. She stretched forth her holy hands" in a
maternal gesture, now, "to take me up" as would a mother, but
also to "embrace me" like a spouse. For, virgin though she
obviously is, she is "far from barren, but the fecund mother of
children, joys born of You, Lord, her husband" (VIII, 27).

Augustine's problem is that he has been trying to "will"
his own conversion, unaware that only God's grace can bring
it about. "Why do you stand in yourself," Continence chides
him, "and so not stand at all?" The expressions are modeled on
Isaiah's challenge to King Ahaz about standing in God or not
standing at all; Augustine has been playing variations of this
theme throughout his *Confessions.*[26] "Cast yourself on Him,"

---

26. See my article, "Isaiah's Mothering God," cited in note 9, above,
esp. 190-91 and 202-4.

Continence urges, "Have no fear. . . . Cast yourself trustfully on Him," then focus on the "delights" — the *delectatio victrix* — promised by "the law of the Lord, your God." Let God do the work; in other words, let him take you up, draw you to himself, empower you to walk, run, fly; carry you, like the lost sheep, home.

Now he hears the child's voice, *"tolle, lege,"* and reads the *capitulum* that among other things calls him away from "rioting and drunkenness . . . chambering and impurities" and urges him to "put on the Lord Jesus Christ": that is, to leave the arena of worldly activities behind in order to embrace, and be embraced by, the life of contemplation; but now, not like some Ciceronian philosopher, but as a "soldier of Christ" (VIII, 11 and 15).

Earlier on, he and his companions had come to the painful realization that their dream of founding a contemplative community must founder on the issue of celibacy: it would be impossible to support a wife and children without working at some remunerative job in the world of "action" (VI, 24). The account in Book VIII makes it plain that Augustine's option for celibacy was clearly bound up with his option for the contemplative life.

Still it would be a mistake to conclude that he envisaged celibacy as holding out no more than this instrumental value. His Cassiciacum dialogues contain some stiff language about the body, the senses, and sensible attractions, but Augustine may have felt such expressions *de rigueur* for the Christian Platonist: they soon soften and even disappear. More significant is his obviously felt conviction, expressed in the *Soliloquies,* that sexual activity adversely affected the tranquillity required for contemplation (I, 17). True, he yearned to behold the supernal Wisdom (a spectacularly feminine hypostasis, like the *Philosophia* of *Acad,* I, 4) in a "most chaste vision and embrace, seeing and holding [her] naked, as it were, no veil intervening": but that Wisdom might rightly act like a woman whose beauty "inflamed [him] with love," and insist he must love her undividedly before she would yield to him (I, 22). Whether from the Beatitudes, from his own experience, or both, Augustine is already convinced that only the single-hearted may hope to see God. And we must constantly remind ourselves that during this epoch Augustine truly believed that the "vision" was something a chosen few (perhaps including himself!) could habitually enjoy, even during "this" bodily life.

Perhaps even more striking in so recent a convert is the unembarrassed candor, the complete absence of puritanical inhibition which he brings to proposing these sexual metaphors for union with God. The fear that Manichaeism succeeded in complexifying his attitudes toward sex seems to have been, after all, unfounded. That lack of inhibition even takes a faintly comic turn: no sooner has Augustine expressed his unshadowed confidence that sexual temptations are a thing of the past for him, when a nocturnal experience proves how wrong he was (I, 25-26). Augustine protests with pain when "Reason" brings the subject up, yet he himself is the author responsible for this surprisingly intimate revelation!

To summarize the lines of Augustine's "ascetical-mystical" paradigm, accordingly, I would first suggest that the man's writings furnish no solid evidence that it was a mask for an unresolved Oedipal conflict; nor that it was a reaction to an unusually stormy adolescence, despite both his parents' fatalistic, *laissez-faire* permissiveness, particularly during his unsupervised Carthage days. Even here we must remember that Augustine quite soon settled into the fidelities of a perfectly conventional marriage.

Despite his years as a Manichee, I can find no convincing *a posteriori* evidence that his ascetical-mystical paradigm grew out of any powerful guilt feelings or genuinely neurotic complexes: the uninhibited overtness of his sexual metaphors, the open candor of his personal revelations betray, rather, a convert remarkable for his matter-of-fact freedom in this area. And his occasional expressions of contempt for the body and sex never come even close, for instance, to the malodorous coinages of Dean Swift's satiric verse; they show up in his earliest dialogues, exhibit all the signs of being "the expected" from a convinced Platonist, but disappear so soon afterward that one wonders whether Augustine's heart was in them in the first place. The "ascetic" paradigm did not, I submit, spring out of any unhealthy revulsion toward either the body or sexual activity as such.

What was it, then, that "fueled" the obvious commitment

which went into Augustine's first adopting, then acting upon and preaching this paradigm? Why did it find so solid a niche among his "real" assents? The texts, I submit, argue consistently in a single direction: from his reading of Cicero's *Hortensius* onward, Augustine was haunted by the possibility that the happiness each one of us seeks (some more desperately than others) could only be found in the vision, embrace, and union with some other worldly being: Divine Beauty. The closest approach, the most consonant preparation one could make toward that happiness during this life, was to embrace the life of contemplation.

If all this be "narcissism" (I prefer calling it a unilateral eudaemonism), Augustine would urge us to make the best of it: he never tires of repeating that the main business of life and of philosophy is to achieve happiness. Everything and everyone we encounter here must be "used" to advance our journey home; only there shall we eternally "enjoy" our Father's House, the Heavenly Jerusalem, our Mother. There is little place here for a nonnarcissistic "object-love," and Augustine's rare signalflares in that direction burn themselves out, alas, all too quickly.

No doubt the *Hortensius* brought him a message to which he was strongly predisposed: some people are even "born mystics." But once that realization "got into" him, it was like a recurrent fever which he could never completely shake off: he could study, debate, marry, rise rung by rung toward the heights of his profession in Carthage, Rome, and finally the imperial city, Milan, but all that life of "action" was only a gauzy scrim, blurring the recognition of his soul's deepest yearning. We must believe the Augustine of Books VI and VII when he dramatizes how unhappy he was; but to believe him, we must try to enter into the psyche of someone who was either a born mystic or, at least, a born contemplative. The "Truth, Truth" he cries out for is not some propositional formula, but that hypostatic (and feminine) reality he refers to in his early dialogues as the transcendent "Beauty of Wisdom" herself.

Finally, in A.D. 386, Augustine found both Ambrose and Plotinus powerfully orchestrating the identical message: that vision, that *spiritual* vision, was his to hope and strive for, were he willing to "cut away everything," "put off the old man," and "put on Christ." To ready himself for God's "embraces," he had to cast off the rival embraces which had so long tied him down.

Yet here, the motivational spur seems to have been less an "ascetical" revulsion toward the body, far more a "mystical" longing for the higher vision. True, we are told that the Plotinus whose *Enneads* so inspired him was "ashamed of being in the body"; but we are told that by Porphyry, a somewhat suspect source on such matters. And while some of the anticorporeal language of *Ennead* I, 6, "On Beauty," finds its way into his earliest dialogues, it is soon tempered by the strenuously anti-gnostic defense of the sense-world Augustine would have read in the later *Ennead* V, 8, "On the Intelligible Beauty." Besides, the Catholica taught that the bodily world was created *ex nihilo:* even "matter" must therefore be "good."

Plotinus's affect toward the body seems to have become more positive and accepting as he aged; Augustine, too, goes through a similar shift, as the force of Christian teaching on creation, incarnation, and resurrection come home to him.[27] But from first to last Plotinus's estimate of mystical union was unwavering: the aspirant to this vision must "turn aside forever from the bodily splendors he used to behold . . . must know them for images, vestiges, shadows, and hasten away toward what they image" (*Ennead,* I, 6, 8). And the aging bishop feels free to quote from that very treatise (in *The City of God,* X, 16): "he who possesses all other blessings in abundance, and does

---

27. These specifically Christian influences seem to have accounted for the "friendlier" relation which, in the later Augustine, binds body to soul. This is true overall, even if the earlier, more inimical relationship reappears when he must do battle against the materialistic notion that the soul is bodily in nature: see *De Genesi ad litteram,* VII, 14, 20ff. But even when that relationship of opposition has been superseded, a remnant of "dualism" still persists: the soul is still conceived of as (what an Aristotelian would call) a "substance," the body being viewed as (a distinct substance which is at the same time) the soul's "instrument." Needless to say, I am convinced that the structure of this hierarchic relationship derives from Augustine's conviction that the soul once existed in a "spiritual" body, and "fell" into a body of the "mortal" kind we all experience as ours; see my *The Origin of the Soul in Augustine's Later Works* (New York, 1987).

not possess this vision, is supremely miserable." In sum, if sexual delight is but a pale facsimile of that loftier vision, embrace, union, Augustine could well think that his daring image put it in its proper place: the traveler who drowses off into such *deliciosae lassitudines* runs the awful risk of never arriving home.

There is, as one of my colleagues at this encounter reminded me, a profound truth embodied in Augustine's attitude toward sexual union. One way of putting it is this: the most intense and meaningful unity humans can experience is spiritual, a unity of minds and wills. But that sort of language has something disincarnate about it; perhaps one could better put it another way: our most intense unity springs from beliefs passionately shared, and of heartfelt loyalties which bind us, less as unfleshed minds and wills than as full-blooded human beings. Augustine was almost certainly right to set our sights on our promised heavenly union with God. But he could, at the same time, have made it clearer to husbands and wives that when they strove to make their sexual union an expression of their reverent love for one another, it could become something in addition to an instrument of procreation, an earthly prefiguration of that ultimate, rapturous union.

Justice, Love, Peace

Eugene TeSelle

Niebuhr and Tillich told us, didn't they, that justice is somehow the expression, form, or further deployment of love? Augustine challenges that assumption.

For him justice stands in a sense *above* love, as referee or judge of its propriety. Whether we take the classic definition of justice as *"suum cuique tribuere"* (to each its own), or Augustine's own statement of the "eternal law" as the divine reason or will which requires that natural order be preserved and forbids its disturbance, or the Ciceronian definition of a republic as a common acknowledgment of right, we find that justice is the criterion of all else.

Yet we should not mistake this for a rigid legalism. Justice stands at the top of the conceptual hierarchy because of its generality. It is a formal, content-neutral norm that makes itself transparent to widely varying data, an abstract formula that is flexible enough to bend to many specific values. And it must bend. One of Augustine's innovations is to extend the *cuique*, the "to each," to God: one gives God what is due by loving God and loving all else in God or because of God.[1] Thus when

---

1. Klaus Demmer, *Ius Caritatis. Zur christologischen Grundlegung der augustinischen Naturrechtslehre*. Analecta Gregoriana, 118, Ser. fac. theol., B, 40 (Roma, 1961), 3-21; F.-J. Thonnard, "Justice de Dieu et justice humaine selon saint Augustin," *Augustinus. Strenas Augustinianas P. Victorino Capanaga oblatas* (Madrid, 1967), I, 387-402.

Augustine speaks of observing the "natural order," he is looking primarily not to the cosmos, as the Stoics might, but to God, the most excellent and honorable in the hierarchy of being and the source of all else.

Hence the importance of *order*, which for Augustine means the proper sub- and superordination of beings on the basis of their value and dignity. Origen had thought that God could not justly cause diversity except in response to free choices made before the creation of the present world. Augustine, by contrast, tried to appreciate the diversity of beings as the result of God's goodness and wisdom. Some of them come into being and then die out, others have a more exalted destiny, but it takes all kinds to make a world, and they should be appreciated in their own natures, their mutual relations, and the ecosystem as a whole (*De civ. Dei*, XI, 22-23).

Order is not static. There is justice when storms rage and flies buzz around our heads. But ordering is also relational. It means seeking our place, finding orientation, gravitating toward it through the affections, and gaining a kind of rest as in an end sought or attained (*Conf.*, XII, 9, 10; *De civ. Dei*, XIX, 12). Thus the task of the human self is to be ordered appropriately, under the God by whom the self is ruled, and over those things which the self should rule.

Even more is involved. The ordering task is not merely that of natural theology, based on the comparative dignity of different beings. Somewhat as Karl Barth would have it, the whole process is presided over by grace, the love of God going forth to illumine the minds and inflame the wills, first of the angels, then of the human family. As a consequence, justice is not only an ideal; it has been actualized from the beginning through the double decision of God and the obedience of the angels, who constitute the City of God, God's true dwelling place, in the heavens. That is the true republic in which full justice reigns; it begets citizens through faith and hope while they still sojourn on earth, and they seek it as their fulfillment, as the only genuine happiness and peace.

Justice, then, would have everything appropriately related, either in its place or seeking its place. It invites inquiry as to what the proper relationships are. Love is not so reliable a guide. "Give order to love within me" was the Old Latin translation of Canticles 2:4. That was a major problem to Augustine. Love ought to be "ordered," for it can be perverse, disoriented, upside down *(ordinatus/peruersus)*. It ought to be "directed," for it can be crooked or "depraved" *(rectus/pravus)*. We do not dwell in the City of God; though we *could* dwell in it, and *should*, it is now only a "might have been." Whether it is only imagery or reflects Augustine's own beliefs (as Father O'Connell would argue), Augustine speaks as though we have deserted the "common good," the God who can be shared by all without rivalry, and have sought individual good, "private property," the *proprium* which is also *privatum*, deprived of the greater good which should have been shared by all. It is the result of self-concern and soon devolves into self-love, accumulation, and ultimately the concupiscence by which our affections pour out of ourselves and are dissipated in the sensible world. Then we have trouble even knowing ourselves, for we have "con-fused" ourselves with things outside ourselves, and the "glue of love" has made us inseparable from them (*De Trin.*, X, 8.11–9.12).

Misdirected love is not solely a personal problem. It is social through and through. In the *Confessions* Augustine evokes the many seductions which lay before him, the cultural conditioning that swept him along. In *The City of God* he catalogues the vivid imagery of the mythmakers, the prurient display of the theater, the blood lust of the arena — and the cynical use of them all by the ruling class, "binding them in civil society in order to possess subjects" (IV, 32). But there is not merely concupiscence, desire for finite goods. There is also the other classic passion, anger, which involves comparison of oneself with others, negotiation of boundaries, fear of losing status, indignation at personal slights, elation at one's own power. It is what animated the old Roman heroism. But of course it also implies rivalry, warfare, domination, civil war, rebellion, and further suppression. The devil is both lion and serpent (Psalm 91:13), dominating through force as well as tempting through subtlety.

Thus Augustine was able to describe, sometimes with indignation, sometimes with irony, sometimes with wry equanimity, the workings of actual human societies, specifically Rome and Israel. Augustine was aware of the role of motivation in political life, and the use of both carrot and stick to reinforce it. Societies are held together by culture, but also by law; and both means of unity are a kind of vestige or diminished reflection of the eternal law of justice. Those who love the eternal God will act in obedience to the eternal law; but on those who love temporal things, temporal laws are imposed. What are the things they love? Life and liberty, health and bodily integrity, family and friends, money and possessions, the status of citizenship. Thus the laws, by arousing fear of losing these earthly goods, maintain the kind of behavior that will preserve the body of society. What they punish is not inward love of these things, but external acts of taking them from others.

Consequently the Ciceronian definition of a republic, as a common acknowledgment of right or justice, applies only to the City of God in the heavens. Other societies must be described and defined in another way, not from justice but from love. It is an insight at which Augustine did not first arrive in Book XIX of *The City of God*. Long before that climactic argument he habitually defined a society as (1) a multitude, to be sure, which is (2) bound together by a bond sometimes described as law, sometimes even coercion, but more often a shared love, and (3) with the result that there is "concord" or "peace." The many are bound together by their common relation to a third factor, shared laws or values, through which they gain not only mutuality, the minimum definition of civil society, but agreement or peace.

And thus we come to peace or concord. In our own day we often think of "just peace" or the biblical vision of shalom, which connotes not only righteousness but restoration and wholeness. But Augustine can easily dissociate peace from justice. Peace may be truly just; but it may not be, for peace is a more inclusive concept, ranging as widely as human love and desire.[2] Agreement may be the peace of conspirators or brig-

---

2. This has been pointed out forcefully by a number of contemporary scholars: Volkmar Hand, *Augustin und das klassisch romische Selbstverstand-*

ands; there can be an unjust peace. Peace is desired even when we know that it is not the enjoyment of total happiness, for it is at least the cessation of conflict, the absence of war. It is a negative good, *nihil aduersi patere,* "suffering nothing adverse" (*De civ. Dei,* XIX, 20; XXII, 30). Perhaps it is only solace in the midst of misery (XIX, 27). But it is still worth seeking.

Augustine's discussion of peace comes only after an evocation of the many miseries of life — the struggle between virtue and vice; the uncertainty of relationships even within the family; the more momentous dilemmas of those who hold public office, under the necessity of acting and yet with ignorance about crucial details; the slaughter of war and its uncertain consequences; the deceptions of the evil demons. In the presence of all of this, peace is much to be desired, if only as a finite and interim goal.

Indeed, Augustine comments (XIX, 11) that peace is a term which is linked in customary usage with *intramundane* experiences and desires, not transcendent ones. Insofar as there is analogy between all degrees of reality, it is most likely to be an *analogia pacis.* And precisely that is what Augustine enunciates, in what German scholars call a "peace tabulation,"[3] in *The City of God,* XIX, 13-14:

---

nis. Eine Untersuchung über die Begriffe gloria, virtus, iustitia und res publica in De Civitate Dei. Hamburger philologische Studien, 13 (Hamburg, 1970), 63-67; Ulrich Duchrow, *Christenheit und Weltverantwortung. Traditionsgeschichte und systematische Struktur der Zweireichenlehre.* Forschungen und Berichte der Evangelischen Studiengemeinschaft, 25 (Stuttgart, 1970), 288-90, 306-11; William R. Stevenson, Jr., *Christian Love and Political Life in St. Augustine and His Modern Interpreters* (Macon, 1987), 35-38; George Weigel, *Tranquillitas Ordinis: The Present Failure and Future Promise of American Catholic Thought on War and Peace* (Oxford and New York, 1987), 31; James V. Schall, *The Politics of Heaven and Hell: Christian Themes from Classical, Medieval and Modern Political Philosophy* (Lanham, Md., 1984), 143.

3. Harald Fuchs, *Augustin und der antike Friedensgedanke. Untersuchungen zum neunzehnten Buch der Civitas Dei.* Neue philosophische Untersuchungen, 3 (Berlin, 1926); Joachim Laufs, *Der Friedensgedanke bei Augustinus. Untersuchungen zum XIX. Buch des Werkes "De civitate Dei."* Hermes. Zeitschrift fur klassische Philologie, Einzelschriften, Heft 27 (Wiesbaden, 1973).

> The peace of the body is the ordered harmony of its parts,
> unmolested by pain;
> The peace of the irrational soul is the ordered repose of its
> appetites, undisturbed by desire;
> The peace of body and soul together is the ordered life and
> health of the living being, without dissolution by death.

Thus far we have a kind of "naturalistic ethic" based on the intrinsic tendencies of irrational beings, seeking their internal peace. Then we have the entrance of freedom, the quest for standards by which to order one's life, and the problems of error and irresolution:

> The peace of the rational soul is an ordered agreement
> between knowledge and action;
> The peace of the mortal person with God is an ordered
> obedience, in faith, to the eternal law.

Mortality is assumed here. It is not bewailed as punishment for sin, though it does mean that human life lives in exile, away from God, and thus one can become a citizen of God's city only through faith and hope.

Only then — after setting a Christian context — does Augustine come to the life of society:

> The peace of human beings is an ordered concord, loving
> one's neighbor as oneself, doing no harm, helping wherever
> possible;
> The peace of the household is an ordered concord of
> command and obedience among those who live together;
> The peace of the city is an ordered concord of command and
> obedience among citizens.

We are told not to misunderstand the character of this commanding. All command *(imperare)* must be caring *(consulere)*, and in this sense it is not domination but service. But command it is. Even without sin there would be subjection of wives to husbands and children to parents,[4] and after the entrance of sin there is inequality and even slavery. Augustine also reflects the

---

4. R. A. Markus, *Saeculum: History and Society in the Theology of St. Augustine* (Cambridge, 1970), 204.

Roman habit of thinking about pacts and the peace that comes
from them as not necessarily bargains among equals; they
could be dictated or imposed, and certainly it was more
"orderly" that way. In any case, with the good use of all these
things, one can arrive at the goal:

> The peace of the celestial city is the supremely ordered and
> supremely harmonious association of enjoying God and each
> other in God.

Thus there is a possibility, even under the conditions of mortality, that the life of human society could function rightly, with
due acknowledgment of the appropriate order. When pagans
criticized the Christian ethic, Augustine's first response was to
defend its viability (*Ep.* 138.9ff.), and he outlined in some detail
the character of a Christian society ordered in relation to God
(*De civ. Dei,* II, 19; XIX, 14).

But the *reality* of human peace is something different. The
citizens of both cities share the same temporal goods, using
them badly or well. Note the adjectives: "temporal" is a neutral
designation of the character of finite things and the peace they
can attain; "earthly," *terrena,* is pejorative, designating either the
society which does not live by faith, or the peace which it seeks.
Its concord is *not* called ordered. And yet this earthbound
society and its peace can be shared by citizens of the heavenly
city, first of all because they are born into it through original
sin and share a common mortality, then because they "seek
concord" between the two cities (cf. XIX, 17).

It is in the light of problems like these that Augustine
makes his summation:

> The peace of all things is the tranquility of order, and order is
> the disposing of all things, equal and unequal, giving to each
> thing its place.

Thus justice, giving to each its due, comes back into the picture.
Peace is one of the effects of justice, the appropriate disposition
or arrangement of all things. Peace can include the fact of evil;
but it is still peace. There is no pain without life, there cannot
be conflict without rival beings, there cannot be evil without
the good of finite natures. Even corrupt being has its own

self-consistency, a kind of "ontological peace." It seeks equilibrium, tries to come to terms with itself; it tries to be "pacified"
within itself, even under conditions of deprivation. But this also
means that it finds a new place in the total scheme of things,
still in accordance with the eternal law of justice. Those who
attempt to escape God's order, Augustine asserts with confidence, find that they are still ordered by God. With poetic
justice those who will not be controlled by God find that they
cannot control their own emotions and their own bodies. The
demons fall from heaven and find their place in the stormy
realm of the atmosphere. By a kind of moral physics, they
gravitate to the appropriate place in the scale of value. Even
disorder is ordered, and Augustine is confident that God permits evil only because equilibrium will be maintained and good
can be brought out of it.

Augustine not only emphasizes what the two cities can
share — human mortality, temporal goods, harmony among
human wills, even the peace of the earthly city — but tries to
identify and delimit what it is that is finally irreconcilable between them. The answer is not surprising, but when it comes
its specificity is helpful. The *differentia* is worship, *latreia*. The
City of God cannot have "common laws of religion" with the
earthly city.

One possibility that springs to mind is the tolerant secular
state which avoids interference in matters of religion — and
keeps religion from interfering with its functions. Augustine
understood such things. Earlier in his career (about 396-99) an
official had written to him worried about dealing with a desert
tribe which swore oaths by their local deities. Would he be
violating the warnings of I Cor. 10 about eating meat offered to
idols, or, worse yet, the command of Deut. 7:26, "You shall not
bring an abomination into your house, lest you become
anathema like it" (*Ep.* 46)? He answered that it is one thing to
swear an oath, another thing to keep an oath; all that is shared
is the oath itself, not the erroneous understandings with which
it is made. The empire's boundaries are kept secure through
such oaths made with barbarians (*Ep.* 47).

But in the nineteenth book of *The City of God* Augustine's
vivid recollection of his own historical setting floods back in

upon the abstractness of theory. The City of God has had to dissent, and make itself a nuisance, and bear the hatred of the earthly city, until it is conquered by its numbers and the many signs of divine favor. Now prophecy is being fulfilled, for the true God — the God of the Hebrews, whom even the pagan oracles had to acknowledge — is being worshiped from the rising to the setting of the sun. Once again Augustine subsides into political theory and enunciates his alternative definition of a republic, contenting himself with a description which can apply to all the nations and empires of the world and take into account their changes of ethos. After some more grumblings about how such societies are devoid of true justice, and how their virtues are really vices if they are not referred to God, he comes once again to his main point: even those who are alienated from God have a peace which is not to be taken lightly, for as long as the two cities are mingled they share the same peace. Although it is the peace of Babylon and they are exiles (and once again Augustine seems agitated by the spiritual differences between the cities), Jeremiah had told the exiles in Babylon to seek the peace of the city where they were, and to find their peace in it. The closer Augustine comes to defining the field of temporal action, the more he is aware of their conflicting loves and conflicting worship, and the more conflicted he himself seems to be. His own resolution is to look heavenward to the eternal peace of the celestial city, leaving to later centuries the task of developing the varied suggestions he had offered.

Thus Augustine, even while pointing us to the shared peace of temporal life, seems to abandon us without giving much guidance. We can relapse into one of the earlier stages of his inquiry — into an Augustinian idealism emphasizing the eternal law of rightly ordered love, which may be overly confident of the rightness of both its own motives and the results of its actions;[5] or into an Augustinian realism, which can indeed

---

5. This feature of Augustine's thinking about government and war has been pointed out by Frederick H. Russell, *The Just War in the Middle Ages,* Cambridge Studies in Medieval Life and Thought, Third Series, 8 (Cambridge, 1975), 18-19, 37; John Langan, "The Elements of St.

be found in his description of the many loves of an errant humanity, but which, if it allows itself to be captured by this horizon, easily becomes cynical *Realpolitik;* or into an Augustinian indifferentism, which, in looking to the ultimate and lasting end of the City of God which it possesses in faith and hope, not only finds finite goods paling by comparison, but regards it as a matter of indifference under what regime one lives (*De civ. Dei,* V, 17).

Augustine's is not a foolishly sentimental view of peace. His description of it is at a high level of generality, one that tries to take the full range of pain and evil into account. Peace is the end for which wars are waged, and peace may be broken for the sake of a peace more to one party's liking. Evil and pain are always parasitic upon the goodness of being, which they presuppose; but they are still evil and pain. Augustine expects for sinners an eternal death, the death in which death never dies (*De civ. Dei,* VI, 12), the death which holds the soul *in* the body against her will and pains the soul *with* the body (XXI, 3). But even this unending conflict presupposes a union of parts, and to that extent a peace — but a peace which is not desired.

On a less eschatological plane, Augustine can envisage ongoing conflict — the spiritual warfare between the two cities, the physical warfare of realm against realm, civil war within realms. Although he wants to avoid the Manichaean assumption that both good and evil are tangible forces, clearly identifiable within the field of existing things, he does not suppose that everything is for that reason peaceful. His theory can take in stride the "Manichaean" character of much of our political rhetoric, with its seemingly unbridgeable differences. The Soviet Union was called the Evil Empire, and in more sober language it was accused of being totalitarian in principle. When KAL 007 was shot down, this was taken to be not an understandable accident but a barbaric act, clear evidence that the Soviets were a breed different from ourselves.

Augustine's Just War Theory," *Journal of Religious Ethics,* 12/1 (Spring 1984), 24-28; and William R. Stevenson, Jr., *Christian Love and Just War: Moral Paradox and Political Life in St. Augustine and His Modern Interpreters* (Macon, 1987), 107-12.

Enemies may really be out there. Reinhold Niebuhr accused the West in 1940 of being unable to believe "that a resolute foe might be intent upon its annihilation or enslavement," and commented:

> It betrays something of the ethos of the bourgeois trader who is certain that he can always buy off his adversary as a last resort and who is convinced that there is no conflict of interest which cannot be resolved in some kind of a "bargain."[6]

And yet there are strikingly non-Manichaean political phenomena. Augustine would not be surprised by such things as the Hitler-Stalin pact, and Low's classic cartoon in which they greet each other: "The scum of the earth, I believe?" "The bloody assassin of the workers, I presume?" We saw late in the 1980s accommodation between the U.S. and the U.S.S.R., Iran and Iraq, Cuba and South Africa. No antagonism seems so final as to preclude negotiation, détente, trade, even alliance.

We have all experienced, and probably have practiced, Manichaean politics in our own spheres of influence. It is standard operating procedure to identify, stereotype, scapegoat, and discredit the person or group responsible for this or that problem. But then we may overhear what is being said about our own group, the contempt in which we are held, the falsehoods uttered about us, the lack of perspective in interpreting what we say or do. Then we feel violated, dismissed as nonpersons, made invisible, having no other significance than as bywords in someone else's harangue.

Moreover, anyone with a few years' experience in real politics has learned that opponents in one controversy may be allies in the next one; thus it is better not to burn any bridges. Indeed, one of the sobering things about growing older is to recognize the political character of potentially all human relationships, such that one cannot unreservedly despise — or trust — anyone. Therefore, recognition of difference becomes the point of diplomacy, and of domestic politics.

In a sense it is easier to have robust opponents than to

---

6. Reinhold Niebuhr, *Christianity and Power Politics* (New York, 1940), 124.

hold everything within one's own power. Augustine appreciated the argument of Scipio Nasica that Carthage should not be destroyed, because fear of a powerful rival would deter the growth of civic vices (*De civ. Dei,* I, 30-31). How, indeed, shall we deal with defeated enemies? The Augustinian principle is to "love the sinner but hate the sin." Germany got the Marshall Plan, subsidies for the Christian Democrats, and NATO. Pu Yi, the "Last Emperor" of China, said in an interview:

> The Communist Party is so great that it does not annihilate the person physically, in the flesh, but rather annihilates mistaken ideas. And so, it made me distinguish truth from lies. I was re-educated. They treated me very well.[7]

Augustine would understand. He urged an official to "persecute the crime but liberate the human being" (*Ep.* 153.3). He became convinced of the rightness of coercion when he saw how grateful former Donatists were for being freed from long-standing custom and being brought to their right minds (*Ep.* 93.17). He was sure that love cannot go wrong, even if the means seem harsh, when it begins correcting error.

Yet then we are reminded of Kant's comment that love is easy, it is justice that is difficult — the justice that acknowledges the other and respects the other's judgments and decisions. Once again we find that love needs to be guided and channeled by justice.

After such considerations of the *scope* of conflict and peace, love and justice, let us examine more closely Augustine's understanding of peace, especially as it is sketched in Book XIX of *The City of God,* and bring it into conversation with contemporary political thinking. Repeating what was said earlier about society and peace, we can pick up at least the following characteristics:

1. Peace is understood within a pluralistic and dynamic ontology, as involving such a multiplicity of beings (or diverse parts of a single being) that order and association and peace are not a foregone conclusion. All things have dynamic tenden-

---

7. Eduardo Galeano, "New Clothes for Pu Yi," *The Nation* (June 25, 1988), 904 (based on an interview in 1963).

cies still to be fulfilled — in self-consistent development, in the satisfaction of desires, in right relation with other beings. There is potential or actual conflict among them. Peace will be the resolution, if not of full-scale conflict, at least of unease, longing, threat, deprivation. No wonder it is desired.

2. Peace between two or more components is mediated by a third factor which they share in common. It may be shared values, shared objects of desire or loyalty, or shared laws given by some authority.

3. The result is rest, tranquility, concord — a subjective state in which desires are fulfilled or at least fears are put to rest. Peace is an end sought, and quiet and concord are the feelings appropriate to the attainment of that end. Of course it may be only a tentative and provisional rest, interrupted by bad dreams from within or war trumpets from without.

The crucial phase is the second, the process through which plurality, difference, conflict come to resolution in some kind of equilibrium. We find three factors (thus the second phase needs to be analyzed into three parts): the ordering process, the values shared, and their distribution to all concerned; or, to put it another way, the "constitutive," the "substantive," and the "distributive" aspects of life in society.

a. How does order come about? Truces and treaties seek mutual benefits through the cessation of hostilities or the undertaking of joint action. Modern social-contract thinking tries to trace (if not temporally, at least conceptually) this ordering process, assuming an initial diversity of wills and interests, then showing how cooperative arrangements come into being with general consent. Game theory tries to specify the various trade-offs between self-interest and cooperation. Augustine's language has some similarities with these modern kinds of analysis, especially his emphasis on consent and shared values. And social-contract theories share with Augustine the problem of bringing harmony out of multiplicity, rivalry, and unhappiness. They try to explain the rise of society, the state, or alliances out of a threatening situation — one in which, furthermore, irrational inclinations and conflicting interests must be brought under mutual control. For Hobbes the initial problem is the brutishness of the state of nature; for Locke it is rivalry and envy over property; for Rousseau the common vulnerability of humankind. But in each case the social contract arises as the agreed solution to a problem, and it is valued not so much as a positive source of happiness but as an alternative to worse misery.

Augustine's view of society — and of the peace that grows from it — is different from social-contract theories in that his conceptual model is not a pact among equals but command by an authority. This should not be surprising. Historians of ancient Israel have shown that one of the models for its language about the covenant was the "suzerainty treaty" imposed by conquerors. Even in a command structure, however, the preferences and desires of those who are subject to authority cannot be ignored. Game theory can be applied not only to independent bargainers but to the relation of those governing to those governed. Those governing have both the means of coercion and control over certain benefits which they can offer to the society; their dilemma is how to mix coercion and reward, whom to compel and whom to buy off. The governed must respond to moves made by those governing, and their concern is to avoid punishment and gain the benefits that are offered without giving up more than can be gained. But there will always be some concessions from above, and some degree of consent from below.

When we reach this point, we recognize that Augustine's own formulations may be more reliable as a descriptive tool, less misleading, less ideological, than those of the social-contract theory. A consensus is more likely to be imposed by some hegemonic power (a ruler, a conqueror, a dominant class, or a revolutionary class) than to be arrived at in a fully open and participatory way. In addition, no ruling group willingly gives up power, as Reinhold Niebuhr saw in formulating his original version of Christian realism, and therefore revolutionary pressures, with all their excesses of passion, are likely to be needed. The hope is that the insurgent group will be the bearer of values that are more inclusive, more humane, and more just than those of the power being displaced. But the point is that consensus arises out of frustration and conflict, and while it may be developed through negotiation and contract, it may also be im-

posed by some hegemonic power or marketed by some fran-
chising party. The process, being driven by strong passions,
may lurch from one domination to another. Indeed, it often
happens that leaders will not seek peace — or their constituents
will not let them — until their seriousness has been demon-
strated in an overt trial of strength. And if peace is generally to
be sought and treasured, it is still tentative and provisional. The
demands of justice may require that peace be disturbed for the
sake of a better peace, if not by war, coup, or revolution, at least
through "dissent" and "struggle."

Are there alternatives to domination as the source of
order? When we are thinking normatively, we feel obliged to
offer some alternative to the use of force. The one most often
heard is the model of interaction and negotiation, contract and
treaty, rule of law, "proceduralism." If nothing else, it has the
backing of prudence — the recognition that individuals,
groups, and states are more likely to observe commitments that
they themselves have made, and the recognition, furthermore,
that it is more consistent, more equitable, and more predictable
all around if the parties play by the same rules.

Yet proceduralism is subjected to criticism from both the
left, for placing excessive confidence in "formal" equality and
ignoring differences in power, and the right, for its indifference
to "substantive" issues of right and wrong. Another answer,
coming from both the socialist and the Catholic traditions, is
participation, as being the only adequate expression of the
dignity of human agency. It means a devolution of power to
smaller, more participatory groupings in politics, the economy,
and wider social life.

But what if people have other things to do with their
evenings, as Oscar Wilde quipped? Herbert Gans has recently
suggested that people seek not participation in government —
or in the large-scale organizations that have come to characterize the private sector as well — but evidence that these structures are *responsive* and truly *representative*.[8] They recognize that
government can do things that they themselves do not do. But

---

8. Herbert J. Gans, *Middle American Individualism: The Future of Liberal
Democracy* (New York, 1988), 113, 123.

they expect government to act as though its powers are delegated to it and its task is to be attentive to their situation. And that, experience shows, is not always the case. Despite all our attempts at legitimacy we are often left with partisanship as the basis of order.

b. Augustine's discussions of society and peace emphasize consent and consensus — two meanings of the same word, both acknowledgment and the unity that comes from it.

According to Augustine's revised definition of a people, one need only look at what it loves in order to see what kind of people it is (*De civ. Dei*, XIX, 24). What is it that they share? It need not be a single thing or a single concept or ideology. It may be a complex myth, or a complex of myths, as numerous as the deities of hearth and field and forum that Augustine satirizes in *The City of God,* or the slogans which successive emperors placed on the coinage to characterize their reigns. It may be an ideal of, say, heroic achievement or public spiritedness which needs to be incarnated in a succession of heroes or political leaders; hence the importance of aristocratic "excellence" or republican "civic virtue," which cannot simply float in a Platonic realm of ideas, cannot be deposited in a shrine, but must live in the people, one by one. It may consist of what we call individual or private values, those of life and health, family and property; but they are shared not only because most people have them or seek them, but also because they are valued in an ideology of freedom or interdependence, competition or sharing. It may even consist in a process, a task, a seeking after appropriate ends or the best ways of realizing them.

Sociologists still debate how to define and identify "community." Is community a sharing of beliefs and values? Is it a sharing of commitments, purposes, virtues, habits of the heart? Or is it less grandiose, simply a sharing of the same turf, "common ground," the place where my needs and interests and anxieties are most likely to be shared with others and most likely to lead to common solutions; perhaps even a shared situation or predicament, within which all must learn to dwell together?

Augustine has an interesting "economic" suggestion about why a community of values is important and even necessary. Anything that is apprehended and enjoyed spiritually, he says, can be enjoyed *together with others,* and it is *not used up* in the process of enjoyment (*Solil.* I, 13, 22; *De lib. arb.* II, 14, 37). Such moments are to be treasured in the midst of a world in which scarcity, competition, rivalry, and consumption are the most tangible facts. At the origins of civic culture may lie the public spectacle, the potlatch, bread and circuses — a gift freely given to all who will come, a donation not based on bargaining, but which obligates the recipients all the more strongly and sets a standard which must be met or surpassed by all who aspire to status and power. If we can pause together to praise a hero or crown an athlete, offer a sacrifice or salute the flag, thrill to the enunciation of a noble ideal or join our voices in celebrating it, that in itself is remarkable, a dim intimation of the vision, joy, and rest which for Augustine, of course, can be found only in the City of God. These are moments of happiness which are not based upon isolated consumption but draw us ecstatically out of ourselves.

Even the apparent exceptions prove the rule. Pentheus is torn apart and consumed by the Maenads, but even this mediates an ecstatic unity. According to René Girard's remarkable theory[9] that "scapegoating" is at the core of human culture, rivalry, emulation, and competition for the same object imply at the same time a unity among the rivals, an obliteration of their difference, a communion in the object. Therefore, the conflict between *communion* and *rivalry* is resolved by transferring all the guilt of rivalry to the scapegoat and uniting in ritual aggression, so that the community can redefine itself and dwell in peace. The grandeur of public spectacles may involve vast expenditures, not only of goods or of sacrificial animals, but also of human lives, either directly or through expropriation or deprivation. More often than we like to think, this may be the logic of community.

Thus it makes a great difference what it is that unites us and how, whether it unites by excluding or by including. There are always risks in specifying the common good, for it is usually

---

9. René Girard, *Violence and the Sacred,* translated by Patrick Gregory (Baltimore and London, 1977), still remains the basic presentation of his theory.

specified over against the cultural values, the weal, or the mission of other groups. Then it becomes an idol, a finite deity. These shortcomings of talk about the common good suggest that inclusiveness is an important formal characteristic of any shared vision, any social peace worth having. And inclusiveness is not only a negative criterion, breaking down narrow or premature specifications of the common good; it is also a positive indication of the field of vision — who is involved, how one is to relate to them, even what goods may be involved.

Let us turn to a different notion of community, the minimal one of shared turf, shared needs and interests and concerns. There is nothing wrong with focusing attention on these; indeed, for Augustine they are the proper field of political life. He lists the tangible values of life and health, freedom, family and friends, citizenship and reputation, wealth and property. Love of these things, and fear of losing them, he suggests, is what binds society together in peace. We understand such a list of shared goods. Ours would also include political goods like civil rights, access to the ballot, and defense from violence, social and economic goods like roadways, public utilities, education, and health care, and environmental goods like unpolluted air and water and a protective ozone layer. The European countries especially have developed a political culture in which such goods are seen as the public's business, to be protected or provided because there are human needs to be met and human tendencies to be fostered.

Out of that culture comes the down-to-earth definition of the common good offered by John XXIII, which has received widespread assent: it "embraces the sum of those conditions of social life by which individuals, families, and groups can achieve their own fulfillment in a relatively thorough and ready way." Public goods are not limited to political rights and procedures, for social and economic goods may also be needed for human fulfillment. But this implies that government has access to those resources, at least through regulation, if not through taxation or ownership. Such an implication is met with alarm by those who champion self-denying government, or consider some aspects of life to be intrinsically beyond the bounds of government, or view economic development along capitalist lines as so great a public good that it is not to be hindered by talk of economic and social rights. There is, to be sure, a difference between political rights *against* the state and economic or social claims to benefits *from* the state, to say nothing of a middle range of expectations for "quality of life" that will be protected *by* the state. But public intervention may be required by the nature of human needs, not only those that will always be with us but also those that are created by the character of modern society. These needs may be such that provision of certain goods is the precondition for participation in the very life of society, or to keep some institutions from invading and controlling other institutions.[10]

Whatever our notion of community, we must remember that not only concord but also dissonance follows from an Augustinian perspective on society. What social psychologists call the "relative deprivation" theory is Augustinian through and through.[11] People are unhappy about their condition not absolutely but by comparison with what others have (their "comparative reference group") or with what they might have (their standard of comparison, the "normative reference system"). It is often noted that people can be poor but not know what to call it, that there is not a housing problem until people are told about it; consciousness is important to the dynamics of human life. Revolutions are most likely to occur in times of rising expectations, when poverty or oppression do not seem hopeless and irremediable, or when the dynamics of change are breaking up customary inequalities and people begin to suspect that they have a right to more. Moralists can caution them

---

10. Cf. David Hollenbach, *Claims in Conflict: Retrieving and Renewing the Catholic Human Rights Tradition* (New York, 1979), 31-32, 198-99, and the opposing views expressed by George Weigel, 200-201, 366-68.

11. The classic discussion of relative deprivation is in W. G. Runciman, *Relative Deprivation and Social Justice* (Harmondsworth, 1972), 10-35. Extensive analyses by social scientists include Ted Robert Gurr, *Why Men Rebel* (Princeton, 1970); Melvin J. Lerner and Sally C. Lerner (eds.), *The Justice Motive in Social Behavior: Adapting to Times of Scarcity and Change* (New York and London, 1981); and John C. Masters and William P. Smith (eds.), *Social Comparison, Social Justice, and Relative Deprivation: Theoretical, Empirical, and Policy Perspectives* (Hillsdale, N.J., 1987).

against envy, and philosophers can wax eloquent about "ressentiment" and the differences between noble souls and their valets. But politicians had better attend to the hopes and goals that are bruited about in the society, the comparisons that are made, the sense that people have of where they are in relation to other groups and to others in their own group, and their efforts to correct the situation on their own or in concert with others.

Michael Walzer's *Spheres of Justice* has reminded us of a number of different kinds of goods that are widely shared in our society, each of them tending to generate its own criteria of justice — its own principles, that is, of distribution, not in the economic sense of the term but in the traditional sense of "giving to each what is due." And thus we come to another aspect of social ordering and social peace.

c. What are the rules of distribution, who makes and administers them, and for whose benefit is it done? Augustine's answer, as we saw, is clear: peace is an ordered concord of command and obedience. Some are in charge, but their commanding must be caring, not domination but service, taking into account each one's status, need, or merit. In this way public goods are distributed or access is gained to them.

Of course the market can be the standard of distribution, such that whoever wants something badly enough and manages to pay for it can get it. We in Tennessee have pioneered in hospitals for profit as well as in prisons for profit, offering to take from states and counties the responsibility to administer the corrections system. And there are legal theorists who distribute rights according to costs and benefits.

Still, there are always aspects of life in which distribution is accomplished not through the market but in other ways. In every society there is a kinship system, and among its features is a customary way of "exchanging" or "distributing" mates between families or clans. Sometimes even this distribution is on a market basis, as when dowries are paid; but generally it is far more complex than that. In our own culture we have our nonmarket procedures, not only for mate selection but for the distribution of offspring (through family planning) and for the "nationalization" of family life through laws governing abortion, sterilization, or contraception.

Even the market, however, presupposes social institutions. Neo-Marxists and neo-Ricardians point to the distribution that occurs not through exchange but through prior social relations and the power that comes from them — distribution that occurs not in rent but in land, not in income but in wealth, not in wages but in division of labor. And those who look to the market find themselves pressed toward normative considerations. The descriptive notion of "efficiency" (a distribution which cannot be changed to make some better off without making others worse off) generates a policy norm, that inequities of distribution are justified only if they are to the benefit of the least favored.[12] Indeed, the legal structure regularly tries to accomplish this through regulation, or redistribution, or justification of policies which seem to accomplish just the opposite (e.g., supply side economics, or the allocation of credit to corporate takeovers rather than the construction of affordable housing) by arguing that this will be their ultimate consequence. The criteria may vary: need, desert, social contribution. The mechanisms may vary: deconcentration, public or private administration. The goals may vary: equality of opportunity, or a means-tested level of subsistence, or an entitlement given to everyone, or access to collective goods (such as public transportation or community clinics), or widespread distribution of assets and power to all. But such issues are raised by the character of the market itself, and many of the issues of just distribution come to a focus in "political economy."[13] But it would be misleading to suppose that the issues of distributive justice are restricted to the market and state intervention.

Can some of the problems of distribution be left to the life

---

12. John Rawls, *A Theory of Justice* (Cambridge, Mass., 1971), 68-80.

13. Perhaps the most impressive analysis of distribution, across the whole range of human societies, is Gerhard E. Lenski, *Power and Privilege: A Theory of Social Stratification* (New York, 1966), which argues that the degree of inequality in societies varies with the size of the "surplus" to be distributed. This means that the main variable is technology, which in turn influences the economy, politics, and the distributive system. It also means that coercion becomes increasingly important in maintaining whatever inequalities exist in a society (pp. 435-552).

of society, apart from the state or the market? Michael Walzer not only traces various spheres of life, each of which generates its internal criteria of just distribution, but, more to our present point, suggests the overarching goal of what he calls "complex equality," one in which the many small inequalities will not be amplified by being reflected in other spheres and gaining inappropriate kinds of power. Thus he formulates an "open-ended distributive principle," that no social good should be distributed merely because people possess some *other* social good.[14] In other words, political advantage should not automatically accompany a white skin or a New England (or Texas) pedigree or a stock portfolio.

There is widespread concern that a politically just society might limit the full exercise of individual ability. But it is often phrased in such fashion as to imply that an unrestricted market, personal wealth, or private patronage is the only adequate guarantee of creativity. A pluralistic sense of the spheres of life can help to de-commodify *and* de-politicize our conceptions of initiative, achievement, and fulfillment. Alasdair MacIntyre suggests that the life of society is made up of a variety of "practices," that is, "coherent and complex form[s] of socially established cooperative human activity." Each kind of practice is directed toward goods internal to that form of activity — football, architecture, farming.[15] And he differentiates practices from the institutions which sustain them and administer them, for institutions are concerned with "external goods" — money, career, status, power. Picking up this theme from MacIntyre, Christopher Lasch has drawn a conclusion similar to Walzer's:

> A community consists of a diversity of practices, and its public life ought to nurture these practices, to encourage the widest possible diversity of practices, and to check the influences that tend to corrupt them.[16]

14. Michael Walzer, *Spheres of Justice: A Defense of Pluralism and Equality* (New York, 1983), 20.

15. Alasdair MacIntyre, *After Virtue: A Study in Moral Theory* (Notre Dame, 1984), 187.

16. Christopher Lasch, "The Communitarian Critique of Liberalism," *Soundings,* 59.1-2 (Spring/Summer 1986), 71.

The task is then to keep alive the possibility for citizens to undertake a variety of practices, and especially to be sure that none of them gains a monopoly or undue influence.

Yet it would be most unrealistic to conclude an exploration of Augustinian perspectives on society with such expectations of just distribution devoid of special pleading, favoritism, or monopoly. To call for an end to class domination or a political spoils system is to identify the problem, not to resolve it. Despite the possibility of consensus, we should never be surprised at injustice and dissension, whether it is the result of official corruption, the exploitation of loopholes, or society's neglect of whole segments of its own members.

Augustine affirmed the finite values whose sharing and attainment mean peace. They can be willed by the Christian, whose love for God and obedience in faith mean that the peace of the household, the peace of the city, and peace between cities will be sought in an orderly way. A kind of "reality principle" is at work in Augustine's discussions of peace, asking us to attend both to the natures of things (all the way from the irrational to the angelic) and to the conditions under which they can live with each other. It is a challenging task, but one worth taking on, and not out of keeping with Augustine's Platonism, which, far from implying a dualism betwen infinite and finite, or inward and outward, makes a place for many degrees of being and many modes of interaction among them.

Augustine's theory is one that treats finite goods, even though they are transitory, with respect. To be sure, they are ambivalent, for they can be "referred" to different ends. But that does not do away with their importance as shared values, a basis of common endeavor despite the diverse motivations or commitments of those who participate in human life together. And his ultimate loyalty, far from diminishing interest in finite achievements, promises not only motivation and staying power to undertake them, but perspective from which to affirm them in appropriate measure.

The Story of an Encounter

John R. Muether

Nineteen eighty-seven marked the 1600th anniversary of the baptism of St. Augustine of Hippo. The occasion was accompanied by a great deal of reflection in western Christianity on the life and thought of the one whom many consider its greatest theologian. This reflection provoked some questions about Augustine's influence in the Church. Has he been a bane or a blessing? Has his role been generally exaggerated? And what does a fifth-century bishop from North Africa have to teach the modern world?

These questions interested a gathering that constituted a conference of twenty scholars at The Union Club in New York City on October 27 and 28, 1988. Although the conference commemorated the anniversary a year late, the enthusiasm clearly had not waned. Not all in the group were Augustine scholars. But all of the participants shared a common interest in the question of the meaning of Augustine's thought for the Christian faith in the modern world.

I. GOD, LOVE, AND KNOWLEDGE

According to William Babcock of the Perkins School of Theology, Southern Methodist University, a key to Augustine is understanding how he connected loving and knowing. Contrary to the contemporary habit of setting rationality against emotion, the two went together for Augustine. Said Babcock: "Knowing was, for Augustine, the mode for loving the eternal. It's how loving attains its object." This means something about knowing, Babcock continued, since for Augustine there is no knowing the eternal which is not loving the eternal. "Augustine supposed that knowing which did not include loving the eternal would not really have us knowing at all. Not only is knowing love's mode of attaining its object but also knowing itself is deficient without the loving which alone brings us the appreciation of who it is we know."

The conference moderator, Richard John Neuhaus, now director of The Institute on Religion and Public Life, was impressed by Babcock's formulation. "I was struck at how sharply you put it: That to know God is to love God." It reminded Neuhaus of Robert Jenson's recent book on Jonathan Edwards, *America's Theologian*. "Edwards had a very similar formulation: if you do not love God above all, you do not love God at all, and it is not God you love. To know God is to love God," Neuhaus reinforced.

Babcock said that he resisted the temptation to refer to Anders Nygren and the influential schema on agape and eros that Nygren had entrenched in theological circles. But Neuhaus encouraged him not to resist that temptation.

In response, Babcock felt that he found Nygren unhelpful. "The more I thought about it the more difficult it became for me to see how to use Nygren, and I thought what we really need is to start fresh. As soon as you start separating the subjective and the objective, or the psychological and the ontological, like Nygren does, you are already getting off the track as far as Augustine was concerned. They're mixed together for Augustine, they're not separated out. So I posed the problem without reference to Nygren or to the ways in which Nygren has been discussed."

Eugene TeSelle, who teaches at The Divinity School of Vanderbilt University, sympathized with Babcock's dilemma and went a step further. "Rightly or wrongly, hasn't Nygren been irrelevant to Augustine studies for many decades?"

Robert O'Connell, a philosopher at Fordham University, wasn't so sure. "Once you admit that *cupiditas* [love of transitory things] and *caritas* [love of the eternal] are both forms of love for Augustine, aren't you back to the Nygren problematic? Isn't that what Nygren wanted to say?"

"It's more than that," added Ernest Fortin of Boston College. "As I understand it, Nygren was basically a Kantian, by divorcing love and duty. There is a unity that Babcock is trying to restore to Augustine's thought that is lacking in Nygren. The fundamental issue for Nygren is whether one is always engaged in a war against oneself when one loves God and does what God commands. Is it love if you are doing it willfully?"

Babcock insisted that he didn't like that way of phrasing the problem. "I find it difficult to conceptualize that way. It also seems strange to suppose that one ought not to love God because to love God would be somehow self-interested. Why shouldn't one get some pleasure out of God?"

Neuhaus agreed. "Why shouldn't it be in one's interest to love God? It is the right interest." Neuhaus then sought a further clarification. Is Babcock persuaded that self-interest is something short of "real love"? Or does Babcock argue that Augustine himself never had scruples about the love of God being self-interested?

"Sure, Augustine addressed the question," answered Babcock. "He was interested in why people love God and what's in it for people. That's why I find it difficult. Once you start drawing contrasts between what is self-interest and what isn't, and at the same time label what is self-interested as somehow bad, then what can you say?"

The Problem of Neighbor Love

At this point Gilbert Meilaender of Oberlin College shifted the focus of the conversation: "I don't think it matters very much whether one talks about Nygren or not. But in reading Babcock's paper, one inevitably gets driven to certain questions. One that seems to cry out for an answer is how are we supposed to love these transitory people and things to which we are committed. To what sort of language are we going to turn to talk about how the heart is attached to these transient goods? You show that *cupiditas* is not bad, but it's still *cupiditas* after all.

"When I try to think about Augustine in categories that Babcock suggests I do, I find myself returning to questions that I learned from Nygren to think were important. Namely, what happens to the neighbor? How am I supposed to be committed to that person?"

The discussion moved, then, to the question of whether Augustine's understanding of love for God weakened or strengthened love for neighbor. Does Augustine provide, it was asked, an adequate grounding for the love of neighbor?

TeSelle ventured an answer to the Nygren *agape-eros* dilemma. "Augustine first values God as God and then he desires union with God through knowledge. When you achieve that union, you achieve happiness, joy, and so forth. So desire comes after valuing. Sure it's eudaemonism — we all seek happiness — but that's not the first thing that Augustine says."

Robert O'Connell wasn't sure that love preceded desire in Augustine. O'Connell said: "When in his preaching he tells his people that we must love God for God's own sake, Augustine means that you don't love God for the things that God can give you. So you're not using God for temporal goods. You love God for himself because he is infinitely desirable.

"Yet God made us self-interested creatures. He made us creatures of poverty. Therefore this orientation is his own doing, and there's nothing wrong with it. God himself implanted self-interest.

"Now I have no quarrel with that. But anybody who knows something about love knows that it is only part of the story. When Augustine himself starts wrestling with the problem of using my friend here, you see his discomfort. He knows he's in a bind with that disjunction. And yet his tools aren't plenteous enough to get out of that disjunction."

The solution that Augustine should have found, O'Connell suggested, was available in Aristotle via Cicero. "Aristotle is perfectly willing to admit that, in a true and perfect friendship, I'm going to get pleasure and it's going to be useful to me. But the reason why I love my friend in a true and perfect friendship is not for the pleasure and not for utility, but simply because this is a beautiful person. But I never see Augustine saying precisely that."

David Novak of the University of Virginia questioned O'Connell's interpretation of Aristotle. "In Aristotle, it is very clear that I do not love my friend for what he is, in and of himself. I love my friend precisely because we both love the same thing, which is virtue. In other words, it is because we are both loving that which transcends pleasure and use. I would suspect that Augustine couldn't possibly have adopted that Aristotelian notion because of his notion of a personal God."

Babcock commented that Augustine found in Cicero an outright statement that one loves one's friend as an end in himself. "That's what it means to have a friend. A friend is someone appreciated in himself or herself. And Augustine clearly won't buy that, because it treats the friend as an ultimate value. Augustine believes that there is something beyond that, namely God. And so Augustine transfers the focus from the friend to God. The One valued on his own right and for his own sake is God."

Babcock did concede that Augustine had created a conceptual problem with the second love command, the love of neighbor. "Augustine sets it up this way: *fruitio* [enjoyment] applies to God and *usus* [use] applies to things other than God. But it isn't exactly satisfactory, though, to say that we use our friends. It seems to me that Oliver O'Donovan is right in saying that Augustine tries out the notion of use-love, and it doesn't work. So he gives it up."

"And he ends up in a curious formula," added Robert Markus of the Catholic University. "The attitude toward your friend is *fruitio in deo* [enjoyment in God], which is not so much a formula as an expression of his unhappiness at his own conceptual scheme."

"Let's remember this," interjected TeSelle. "If we're going to kick the *usus-fruitio* distinction around, let's note that it is just a passing phase, if O'Donovan is correct. Augustine tries to find a better formula, either in God, or because of God, or you love God and then love those whom God loves, or you refer love of your neighbor to God, and so forth."

But Gil Meilaender continued to find these alternatives unsatisfying because, he claimed, all of them insufficiently captured the commitment one is to have to the neighbor. "There is something appropriately tyrannical about love for God. God is that sort of being." Meilaender was searching for a love of God that would invigorate rather than sap the intensity of other loves.

Gregory Jones, who teaches theology at Loyola College in Baltimore, suggested that a further distinction would be helpful at this point. He said: "Augustine at times seems to think of God as a dominant end, which does sap the intensity of other loves. But when he talks in some of the other writings about the friend in God, God becomes an inclusive end. People are not relegated to just 'use'; they become proximate ends which are then included in the supreme good."

The question was inevitable in a conversation about Augustine and neighbor love: What about love for enemies? Paula Fredriksen of the University of Pittsburgh wondered how a Donatist would regard Augustine's views about neighbor love.

Joanne McWilliam of Trinity College in Toronto suspected that Augustine redefined love when he talked about love for the Donatist. Augustine had a gift for redefining terms so he could keep using them, she said.

But Ernest Fortin was willing to come to Augustine's defense. "You can't love everybody. That's humanly impossible. Augustine handles that with his discussion of the order of charity. You begin with the people who are closest to you and then you reach out as far as you can. What about the intractable ones? What about the Donatists? Augustine handles them through a notion of discipline. It's an active love. It may be paradoxical in many ways. But what's your alternative?" The matter of the Donatists was dropped at this point, but it would return later.

Babcock concluded this discussion by stressing that Augustine had no practical difficulty with neighbor love. "Maybe Augustine had a conceptual problem with respect to inserting neighbor love into his scheme of things. But I don't see any reason to suppose that he had a problem with regard to loving his neighbor.

"I had at one time started this paper with Augustine's account of the friend's death in Book Four of the *Confessions*. There you have a good case in Augustine of a wrong love, because it loves a human being as if the human being would go on forever, which human beings won't do. Then Augustine says all the things that were wrong with it. And he says blessed are those who love others in God, because they never lose their friends.

"What has happened? The particularity of the relationships is gone. You have to love everyone in God to love him rightly. But you can't get the intensity if you don't have the particularity. As soon as you've got to love everyone equally, you start draining out the intensity of the love of others on the human level."

"Now one more thing," Babcock continued. "You don't have to resort to Nygren or anyone else to get that point, and you don't have to be Augustine to have that problem. A lot of people think we are to love all people equally. They think that's what neighbor love means: ignore the particularity of the specific person and love them all with a depersonalizing love. Augustine does have that conceptual problem; he doesn't know how to represent it. But he didn't have a problem in the actual living of his life. Peter Brown said that Augustine had a genius for friendship."

Friendship in a Hierarchical Universe

Why aren't we friends with God? Robert O'Connell raised that question, and it launched the conversation into some fruitful directions.

For Babcock the answer was simple. The classical notion of friendship is friendship between equals, and there is no sense in which we can be equal to God, according to Augustine.

TeSelle qualified that, but only slightly. Augustine did talk at times about God as friend, the Vanderbilt professor asserted, but, given the nature of the inequality, God is the one who sets the terms of the friendship.

Joanne McWilliam felt that Augustine's inequality with God was related to his problem with neighbor love. "Anyone who has the concept of a hierarchically ordered universe has no choice but to say we use everything short of God, and that's why he gets himself in the bind with the love of neighbor. When God is at the top, everything under God can only be used to attain God. The love of neighbor gets weakened or wiped out altogether."

Graham Walker, who teaches political science at the University of Pennnsylvania, questioned whether there was any biblical alternative to a hierarchically ordered universe. Is an immanentist universe a plausible alternative?

That was precisely the alternative that Paula Fredriksen wanted to explore. "The architecture of Augustine's Neoplatonic universe is set up in such a way that when I am looking at God I have to look at others through the rearview mirror."

Babcock was amused by Fredrickson's imagery, because he believed that the modern alternative to Augustine's Neoplatonic model suffered from the opposite problem. "Among my students, somehow it's built into them that to love God means to love other human beings. If you ask them if it would be possible to conceive God as someone to love even if there were no other human beings around, they're at a loss. They can't imagine such a thing. If Augustine had to look into the rearview mirror in order to see others, my students have to look into the rearview mirror in order to see God. I'm not sure that either alternative is satisfactory."

Ernest Fortin considered it vital to distinguish love and friendship in Augustine: "The notion of friendship doesn't play that prominent a role in Augustine's thought. Charity is never defined as friendship in the patristic era. That's a medieval notion, which came with the rediscovery of Aristotle's ethics.

"This is, of course, the great Christian novelty: Why should you love your neighbor? To be a little bit crude about it, in ninety percent of the cases, the neighbor is actually disgusting, and there is no human reason to love him. If you love your neighbor, it's because God asked you to do that. It's because God loves him. If you love God, you have to love those whom God loves." And so, Fortin concluded, the motivation for love is altogether different from friendship.

Augustine on the Virtues

Were there some parallels between the demotion of friendship in Augustine and the demotion of virtues? That was a question that Duke University's Elizabeth Clarke put on the table, and it prompted a discussion of Augustine on the virtues.

Robert Wilken of the University of Virginia drew a contrast between Augustine and some of his Christian contemporaries. "Ambrose adopted the scheme of the cardinal virtues, which is much closer to the classical model. But when you get to Augustine, the virtues are all transformed into forms of love, as Babcock describes. In effect, the virtues are really dissolved. What troubles me about this profound shift is that once you start talking of the virtues primarily in terms of their end, you're very close to transforming virtue into attitude.

"So one way of interpreting our discussion is that Augustine has given us only an interpretation of the first half of Jesus' twofold commandment to love. I think, as O'Connell claims, that what we have here is the aesthetic-mystical paradigm. When one thinks about the historical circumstances of late fourth-century Christianity and the new ideal of the aesthetic life, it is not all that surprising that these other considerations of temperance, fortitude, justice, and prudence, in their classical sense, become secondary. They begin to lose their content, their particularity, and certainly they are no longer habits."

Karen Jo Torjesen, a historian from Claremont Graduate School, agreed with Wilken: something on the order of a major transformation was happening to the virtues in Augustine. "The classical virtues really have a very distinct social function and content in the *polis*. What we're seeing in Augustine is the interior reflection on and cultivation of the affective part of the person. This is radically different from the social function of the classical virtues."

O'Connell linked Augustine's teaching on virtue to his Neoplatonic roots. "I think Augustine does exactly what Plotinus did in his treatise on the virtues. He's taking the ordinary civic virtues and showing that the higher and more valid form of each of these virtues is dispositional toward contemplation. It was Plato who started that. The virtues in their higher form have not to do with the life of action but with their disposition toward contemplation."

"Let's pursue that," said Gene TeSelle. "Is Augustine really giving up the notion of the civic virtues or simply setting them in a wider, higher, and deeper context?"

"But doesn't Augustine simply sap them of vitality?" asked Neuhaus. "Doesn't he weaken the virtues?"

Context makes a difference here, observed Babcock. "In *De Moribus* Augustine deals successively with love of God and love of neighbor. When he's talking about the former, it is easy to conclude that neighbor love has been messed up, because the virtues show up in the way they do with respect to the love of God. He's not talking about other loves."

Addressing Wilken, Babcock went on to ask: "I don't understand why you would want to say that the virtues are somehow being reduced to or transformed into attitudes. Maybe I don't understand attitude in the way you understand attitude. But I just don't see that."

"Well, I contrast attitude with action or deeds," Wilken replied.

Augustine understood the virtues as dispositions of character, noted Babcock. They are always to some extent dispositions. They include actions but they are not themselves actions.

"They are actions of the soul," added TeSelle.

Richard Neuhaus proposed that the problem of neighbor love could be turned around, and that perhaps the love of God could strengthen the love of neighbor. "Does Augustine make the claim that those who love God first will love their neighbor better as a consequence?"

"Augustine makes various claims," said Babcock. "He claims in *De Moribus* that the cradle of the love of God is love of neighbor. And in his sermons on First John, he'll say that to love the neighbor is to love God."

Augustine also uses the image of a ladder, added O'Connell. "We are going up a ladder, and the first step to loving God is loving the neighbor."

This line of discussion seemed promising to Meilaender, even as he risked contradicting his earlier concern. He noted: "It's true that from one perspective you can think of the love of God as a sapping of the virtues. But you could shift the angle of vision and think of Augustine as giving someone who is overcome by the love of God a way of trying to do justice to these virtues as virtues. We don't just have to write them off as vices, but they remain virtues in a way."

And so which is it? Has Augustine sapped the virtues or has he given them integrity? Robert Markus set forth a solution. Echoing O'Connell's earlier remark, Markus suggested that Augustine "is giving place, within a Christian Neoplatonic framework, to the standard classical virtues."

"So Augustine was putting a Christian spin on that which was familiar?" asked Neuhaus.

"That's how it seems to me," was the reply from Markus.

But that's not quite how it seemed to Fortin. Fortin challenged the assumption that there was one classical notion of virtue. There was more than one, he went on to claim. "Who talks about moral virtue in antiquity? Aristotle. Nobody else talks about moral virtue. In Plato, it's not moral virtue but political virtue. Plotinus picked that up and speaks of virtue as something instrumental. It somehow has to go beyond itself to something higher, whatever that might be. Augustine is tied to that tradition. He has an instrumental conception of virtue. That is not the innovation; the innovation is that this is put in a much more definite Christian context. He can do that because he has the Bible behind him."

"So is that more than putting a Christian spin on it?" asked Neuhaus. "Does it change much of anything?"

"Well, it changes the expression of these virtues," said Fortin. "Love of neighbor would be one of the great differences. No classical philosopher ever said that you had to love everybody. According to classical philosophy, you can command expressions of love maybe, but you can't command love itself; that's a contradiction in terms."

Fortin's comments struck a cord with Gregory Jones. "We need to get away from classical versus Christian virtues. There are at least two strains of the classical virtues, a Platonic strain and an Aristotelian strain. Part of the difficulty here is that you use Aristotelian language about disposition of character to designate what seems to be a much more Platonic account of the place of the virtues within life. That is confusing, and it seems to suggest more unanimity in the classical accounts of virtue than there is."

Arresting Love

If a hierarchical universe is one of the concepts that constrained Augustine to view love in a certain way, Robert O'Connell set forth another image that he considered as basic, and that was *peregrinatio,* or the pilgrimage image. O'Connell: "You're not home till you're home, as Yogi Berra would put it. One of the great things Augustine sees is how we can love someone so intensely that we get the illusion of being home."

"I can think of a thing as good for me, or I can think of a thing as beautiful in and for itself. The latter inspires an almost arresting beholding. That insight — so strong in the *Confessions* — begins to wear thin as Augustine goes along. He gets more and more anxious about the possibility that we might become arrested by that kind of experience. And so he shoves the beautiful into the category of the good, and it becomes part of his order of loves. But I've often wondered if he had awakened one day and said, 'Wait a second, I want to exploit that insight.' One of the paradoxes of being a Christian is that God has made certain features of his world so beautiful that he wanted them to arrest us, so that we would not be in such a hurry on our *peregrinatio.* This is one of the peculiarities of our experience of this world."

O'Connell's problem of arresting love reminded TeSelle of the problem of dominant ends. By the time he wrote the *City of God,* Augustine had reached an understanding of inclusive ends, thought TeSelle. "It's possible to enjoy everything in God, as long as there is a correct perspective on everything. It doesn't arrest you, but you are able to see it within the whole horizon of love for God. The ideal is not a zero-sum, *either* love for God *or* love for these things. It's both."

O'Connell contrasted the idea of arrested beholding with disinterested beholding. "Augustine talks about created things bearing witness to God. To understand them properly is to follow in the line in which they point us. I'm thinking of the *Confessions* where we have the spider weaving its web. It's one of the few cases where a classical author lingers over just such detail. But his attitude is clear: to be arrested here would somehow be a mistake. What he's really asking for is an attitude of disinterested beholding. If you can take that attitude you will see that this creature is good, in and for itself. It's a product of divine art."

"And it's to be loved," added Neuhaus.

II. WHAT DOES TRUTH HAVE TO DO WITH IT?

Up to this point, the discussion had focused on the mandate for Christians to love their neighbor. Some of the ramifications of this mandate came out in the discussion of Ernest Fortin's paper.

Fortin began by outlining the difference between Augustine and his pagan mentors. This is a perennial issue that is not dead by any means, Fortin asserted. "One of its key differences has to do with the fact that Christians are expected to love their neighbor. This is not a completely natural thing," said Fortin.

Neuhaus wondered if Augustine's approach was so different that there was warrant for locating in Augustine a new literary genre. "I think that Ernie very helpfully contrasts the dialogical character of Augustine's pursuit for truth with that of Socrates. In the *Soliloquies*, for example, Augustine does not assume, like Socrates did, that he had the truth, and that now he will tease and play games with others. But rather he thinks that truth and falsehood are somehow within himself. Is this original with Augustine?"

Robert Markus found a clue in the *Confessions*. "I think one underestimates the light that the *Confessions* throws on one's attempt to understand Augustine. I'm thinking particularly of a phrase that I associate with Paula Fredriksen, when she described on one occasion the *Confessions* as 'theology in a new key.'" Markus marveled at the "absolute originality" of the combination of prayer, meditation, and analysis in that spiritual classic. "This is a wholly new kind of literary medium which gives one a kind of mirror to the quality of Augustine's life, his thought, and his feelings. One has this experience every time one teaches a course on Augustine. The *Confessions* is the kind of book which students hardly ever encounter. In literary terms, it's an absolutely novel genre."

"So there is a new thing in the Christian reality," Neuhaus noted. "It is assumed that in being a Christian one is already in confrontation with the fullness of the truth."

Joanne McWilliam observed that Augustine's use of the meat-milk metaphor was useful here. It isn't that Augustine sometimes lies, or that he is willfully holding things back, she asserted. He simply thinks some people are not yet ready for the complete truth.

Robert O'Connell agreed: "One of the great metaphors for teaching is the mother giving milk to a child, so that the child may grow up to eat the food on the father's table. But as soon as Augustine begins to develop that metaphor, he's very sensitive. He'll insist that it is the same food. The mother eats at the father's table, and then that food passes through her system, and so the father's food is the same food that the infant is being fed."

Fortin's contrast between Christian instruction and pagan teaching impressed Graham Walker, who wanted to explore it further. "I wasn't sure I understood your distinction fully. You suggest that Augustine understood that the Christian proclamation was different from what preceded it. But didn't someone like Plato or Aristotle or Socrates think that truth was persuasive in itself, and that it didn't need any embellishments? How is that really different?"

Fortin formulated the difference this way: "Augustine thinks with St. Paul that the Word of God has been spoken with power. It has the capacity to move you as long as there are no obstacles to its effect within you. I don't think you can say that with human truths, truths that have been developed by the human mind without the aid of divine revelation."

Fortin's formulation met with dissent from Robert Wilken: "As I read your paper, I sense that you criticize the pagan philosophers for what they do, but you judge the Christians on the basis of what they say they ought to do. You're using completely different standards."

Fortin considered the charge unfounded. "I don't criticize anybody! I'm not criticizing the pagan philosophers, I'm just telling you what they do. But Augustine does outline a criticism of pagan philosophy in the *Confessions* and elsewhere. What's wrong with these people?, he asks. They're proud; they don't have any humility; they're too snobbish; they're aloof. They distance themselves from their fellow human beings, and they only associate with their own kind. That's why they have to tell lies."

Babcock wondered if Augustine's criticism applied to Augustine himself. "For Augustine, the Bible is a highly ambivalent book. On first reading, it's culturally uncouth, it's morally depraved, and it's packed full of lies about God. No one who understood God would ever say such things. Consequently, one must reject it, which Augustine did. So he becomes a Manichee. But his subsequent interpretations of the Bible respect its ambivalence. He himself understands Scripture to be speaking in a variety of ways, accommodated to different people and to different levels of culture. In fact Scripture itself pushes you along to help you rise above these unsatisfactory and primitive ways of speaking that Scripture itself uses."

There are some things in the Bible that are simply false, Babcock continued. "The false is there to provoke you to an understanding of something else. It's certainly true that with respect to preaching, Augustine prefers clarity. He often says that it is more important that the listener understand than that the preacher be eloquent. But his preference for clarity in preaching doesn't convert to the notion that the Bible is a book whose meaning is always obvious.

"So we don't just have the theologians speaking one way to the populace and another way to the theologians. We have *God* speaking to the populace in one way and in another way to the theologians. It's the same problem that you see among the philosophers."

What then is distinctive about Augustine? Graham explained: "Socrates confronts his students with true things, but he will engage in deception when speaking to others. On the other hand, Augustine believed that all of the levels of biblical truth are compatible with one another. The higher does not contradict the lower. Therefore, the Christian proclaims the same truth to whomever he speaks."

At this point Robert Wilken wanted to cast a vote on the side of the pagans. "I don't think they were arrogant and systematically untruthful."

Robert Markus didn't draw the distinction between truth-telling and lying. Rather, "the fundamental parting of the ways is between a religion that is prepared to make a distinction between the elite and the rest, and this is what Augustine will not stand."

But Wilken remained unconvinced: "That's a very clever way to escape. It's really unjust to say that the matter has to do with the ethics of discourse. Consider the Jews. Augustine is as harsh on the Jews as he is on others, because they too did not have the truth. So the question is not a matter of the formal deficiencies of pagan rhetorical tradition. Augustine felt that this group and these people did not have the truth. That's the primary issue."

Neuhaus asked Wilken if Augustine's opponents thought they had the truth in a way analogous to the way Augustine thought he had the truth.

"The Jews did, the Manichees did, and the Donatists did," Wilken replied. "Now the difference with the pagans is that they did not believe there was a universal revelation that applies to all people."

"But," Neuhaus pushed him further, "isn't that exactly Ernie's point? Isn't that what permitted Augustine to engage in a different understanding of the ethics of discourse?"

"No," replied Wilken. "It just meant that the pagans were not going to make claims about what had happened to people thousands of years before. What it finally comes down to is whether you are committed to an historical revelation. That's of course the difference in Augustine and all the other Christian thinkers.

"By looking at the 'ethics of discourse,' you shove this issue into secondary matters and assume the pagans were living a lie. But they simply didn't feel that they had this kind of universal truth at their disposal. For that reason then, they did not argue the way Augustine did. But it wasn't a matter of whether lies were appropriate or not, or whether one was elitist or not."

Also Wilken said that he was uneasy with the conversation constantly assuming Augustine's perspective: "We don't understand the world that Augustine was living in and the struggles he was involved in if we interpret his opponents only through his own eyes."

Vanderbilt's Jean Bethke Elshtain agreed that there was a problem seeing Augustine's opponents through Augustine's own eyes. But for her that was not the main issue. "What is ultimately at stake is the construction of lies as a way of establishing the political order. Augustine could never sanction something like the Platonic noble lie, a situation in which there is one construction that's available to elite knowers and there are other constructions that they put out for the benefit of those who are incapable of their level of understanding. Sure, he wouldn't read *De Trinitate* to his congregation, but that's not a construction set up to deceive others or to deprive them of understanding. He's got to make some sophisticated and shrewd rhetorical choices to make possible some forms of understanding."

Those rhetorical choices are unavoidable, Elshtain continued, for anyone in dialogue with others. "But what Augustine could not countenance, and in fact explicitly rejected, was the notion that there is some truth over here that I and some others understand, and that I am explicitly going to deny that truth to others, or that I am going to deceive them in explicit kinds of ways for their own good. Augustine totally rejected that."

Augustine's position carried great significance for political thought, Elshtain went on to point out. "There are continuing implications for our thinking about politics — regarding the legitimacy of having an elite of political philosophers or policymakers explicitly constructing and disseminating lies. These lies, however noble, are in order to manipulate the masses towards ends that they are either in principle incapable of understanding or ought not to have in their own possession. It seems to me that Robert Markus quite correctly alerted us to how radical Augustine is in this regard.

"There's an interesting development to this in the history of political thought. Many subsequent political thinkers, such as Machiavelli and Rousseau, assume that Christians are likely to be finicky in a way that Augustine is, and they argue that Christianity is a very bad civic religion. One cannot and ought not to trust it as a civic religion in part because of the kinds of arguments Augustine made."

Wilken held his ground. "I still do not recognize the pagan world in that description."

Eugene TeSelle wondered if the uniqueness of Christian discourse may be related to its message. "It is precisely because Christians have the *one* way of truth that they are able to halt the pagan sacrifices, destroy the temples, and coerce the Donatists. It may be great to have the universal way of salvation, but that has its consequences."

"So is it better to consider Christianity not to be true?" asked Graham Walker.

Neuhaus thought that Walker's question was a very good one, and he carried it further. "It is certainly dangerous to believe that one possesses the truth. And one points to Augustine's treatment of the Donatists as a manifestation. But what's the alternative? Is it the modern notion that pretends that nobody possesses the truth, and thereby avoids the dangers of fanaticism by cultivating the virtue of a relativistic form of tolerance?"

By way of response, Wilken reminded the group that the truth is never distinct from a historical community. "When Augustine gets up against the wall, when people quote to him Cyprian on the other side of an issue, Augustine appeals then to the community rather than to the truth. He doesn't appeal to the truth, because somebody who was in the community, namely Cyprian, had a different truth."

Undaunted, Ernest Fortin continued to press his case for the moral superiority of Augustine over the pagans in the ethics of discourse, and he wanted to frame the difference as sharply as possible. "The issue revolves around moral virtue, which is not required for a pagan philosopher. If you read the pagans, you see that, as a rule, they talk the way Christians don't talk. There's no commitment to the neighbor on their part. That's a major difference."

"That's just false! That's totally false!" exclaimed Wilken.

Neuhaus sought further clarification from Fortin: "What do you mean by saying that they had no commitment to the neighbor? Clearly, there was a commitment to the *polis.*"

Indeed, that was the pagan criticism of Christianity, noted Paula Fredriksen. Christianity was viewed as antisocial, and therefore Christians were accused by pagans of not loving their neighbor.

The philosopher may feel that he has a certain responsibility toward the city, replied Fortin, but it is not moral obligation. "The philosopher simply realizes that you must have cities. There is no existence outside of them. Who wants to go out into the wilderness? So you speak and act in a responsible way." Christianity was, in the beginning, antisocial, Fortin acknowledged to Fredriksen. But he said that it was the genius of the Church Fathers to inject an element of political sense into the Christian scheme. "That's what Augustine did, and this is one thing for which I personally admire him very much."

Neuhaus inquired about the pagan sense of responsibility to the city. "Ernie, are you saying pagans lived certain ways simply to maintain a city; whereas Christians were obligated to live certain ways and that their obligation had moral status?"

"A divinely given obligation," added Fortin. "The pagans had a sense of responsibility toward others, but no sense of moral obligation."

The Theological Interpretation of History

Paula Fredriksen led the group into the exploration of a key hermeneutical issue. "What strikes me about Augustine is that he is developing this incredibly sophisticated and sensitive school of hermeneutics for the biblical text. While he does it, he's letting go of a hermeneutic of history. History is radically opaque. You're not allowed to look at political events and interpret them through the hermeneutic of biblical meaning.

"That is why there's so much attention to love and will. They become the proper arena to discuss the meaning of scriptural texts, and such scriptural discussion is not going to be as socially dangerous as discussing the meaning of an historical event. So history does become radically secular. You can't interpret it theologically at all."

Neuhaus was unsure in what sense history had become secular.

"Secular in that you cannot see a redemptive pattern in current events," asserted Fredriksen. "It's improper to use revelation to interpret contemporary events."

"But," added Gil Meilaender, "you can see through the prism of the two-cities analysis. It's not that you can't say anything about those events. It's that you can't locate divine redemptive activity here."

"But you can't see a pattern of revelation," maintained Fredricksen. "That's what I meant by saying that history is becoming secular. That enables a lot of subsequent developments in Western culture.

"Augustine disallows any kind of correspondence between current political or social events and the ultimate religious reading of existence. You can't hook the two of them up, to put it crudely. The suffering of the righteous does not entail thinking that God is at hand. This is the burden of a lot of the latter part of the *City of God.*"

Neuhaus pressed her on this point. "You said that Augustine excluded the idea of biblical prophecy being fulfilled in this way. But did he exclude the theological reading of the events of his time, in the sense of God's work in history?"

"No, he couldn't do that and be Christian," replied Fredriksen.

Robert Markus expressed the difference in terms of the end of inspired revelation. "Augustine thinks that God is at work in all history, but in biblical history he is not only active but also inspiring the prophets to interpret what he is really up to. That is what stops. Now we know that God is at work, but we don't really know what he's up to."

And so, summed up Neuhaus, "Augustine didn't make revelation contingent upon an interpretation that could be falsified historically. Is that right?"

Recalling Babcock's comments on *cupiditas,* Fredriksen responded: "That's like loving something temporary; you can't bank on that."

Meilaender thought the discussion of Augustine on history and revelation hadn't gone far enough. "Augustine really can say more in a way. The *City of God* is a big book. In Book Five he says that the founding of Rome is an intimation of the truth of the City of God. He is willing to find intimations within human history, but clearly not the sort that he could plot on the graph of God's redemptive activity. There are, for Augustine, at least moments of intimations, though you shouldn't press it too far."

Eugene TeSelle added that there was a theological reason for Augustine not to do what Fredriksen wanted him to. "Augustine allows events in the history of Israel to be significant. But that history is ambivalent, both as its own national history and as a prediction of Christ in which everything will become clear. So once you've got what's clear, you no longer need that kind of national history with its sacral overtones. After Christ, everything is couched in Christian proclamation."

Fredriksen added: "Christ ascends and then it is not until the Parousia, when history is realized and everything is revealed, that we'll know what things really mean. It is as if Augustine throws a train switch, and the train just goes on a different track. The newspaper has nothing to do with the Bible."

Neuhaus was unsatisfied: "But what really has been the big difference? It is certainly not that Augustine has any lesser notion of his historical moment being a working out of divine providence than the era of the prophets. The difference is the authority with which one can claim the discernment of those purposes, after the closing of the revelation. If that's the case, why is history any more 'secular' than it was before?"

Fredriksen contrasted the way Eusebius and Augustine looked at history. "Eusebius could look at an emperor and say, 'This is Isaiah's peace,' but Augustine simply wouldn't do that."

"But no less than Eusebius, he would also say that all this that has happened is part of the unfolding of God's purposes," said Neuhaus.

"But nobody knows what that purpose is," Fredriksen responded.

Paul Hinlicky, editor of *Lutheran Forum*, jumped on the comparison with Eusebius. "Might it not be also that Augustine has a more complex reading of the Bible, with the two cities?

The Bible is not unilaterally the story of the progress of the city of God. From the beginning it is the intermingling of the two cities."

Meilaender continued Hinlicky's thought: "What the two-cities notion provides is a way of thinking, in a secularized way, about all political communities in which we find ourselves. Through the prism of that image we see that none of them is the City of God and that none of them is to be identified precisely with God's purposes. But once you say that, then you can say a lot of theological things about what is happening in the actual empirical communities in which we live. This is exactly what Reinhold Niebuhr did in *The Children of Light and the Children of Darkness*. There are the two cities again. And Niebuhr found an awful lot to say about political communities.

"So it is not that this analysis secularizes and thereby leaves us without anything to say. Rather, it gives us a particular theological vision from which to address ourselves."

Robert O'Connell reminded everyone about the ending of the *City of God*, where the Vandals were knocking at the gates. Augustine reads a great deal of meaning in that, O'Connell insisted: "First, this is supposed to be a great consolation. We can console ourselves with the knowledge that all this has been predicted. But then he brings up the metaphor of the winepress, and he assures the people that these temporal sufferings are the winepress of God, pressing out the pure grape." So there are certain theological meanings that Augustine is able to read out of the secular situation.

But O'Connell added an important qualification. "The one he seems very uneasy about reading is the kind of meaning he has seen work for the churches of the pure, both the Manichees and the Donatists, when they claim to tell who's wheat and who's chaff. The moment you claim that is the moment you're in trouble with Augustine."

Truth, Religious Unity, and Coercion

Karen Jo Torjesen suggested that it was important to understand the ways in which truth, religion, and political power converged at certain historical moments. She began: "Sometime around the fourth century B.C., truth was invented by a dispossessed political party in Athens. Truth in this context was one, and it existed in the form of idea or doctrine. Then around 250 with Decius's persecution, for the first time you have the use of political power to coerce religious allegiance. Around 306 for the first time you have the use of political power to coerce religious unity. With the Council of Nicea in 325 you have the use of political power to coerce religious unity on the basis of idea or doctrine. Finally, with Augustine, for the first time you have the coalescence of political coercion and religious uniformity, because Constantine's interest in religious unity was not doctrinal, it was political, and Augustine's interest in religious unity was doctrinal."

Torjesen admitted that she had been somewhat tongue-in-cheek: "The point is that at some time and for some reason the idea of truth with a capital T was invented. That was a curious historical phenomenon. Augustine believed that doctrine was that which constituted unity. False doctrine broke unity, and coercion was legitimate in order to reconstitute unity on a doctrinal basis." Torjesen did not suggest that Augustine was the first to use truth to coerce religious unity. But that is where she said the progression had reached by the end of the fourth century.

Neuhaus wondered if one could at least grant Augustine some credit for being consistent. "Is there a connection," he asked, "between Augustine's unwillingness to tell lies himself and his doing what is necessary to prevent other lies from being told?"

This formulation troubled Robert Markus, because he did not think it described the terms in which the debate was actually conducted. "The truth doesn't come into it," said Markus. "The fundamental issue remains that the Donatists have broken away from the community. Therefore they have to be brought back."

"But they were brought back because they broke that which constituted communion, which was doctrine," said Neuhaus.

"No!" replied Markus. "If it were a debate about truth, the logical consequence for Augustine would have been that the first people to be coerced were the pagans."

Neuhaus wanted to elaborate on that: "The pagans were not culpable in the sense that people who claimed to be Christians were. They also couldn't imperil the truth in a way that Christians, who had partial participation in the truth but had distorted it, could. Therefore the Donatists were a threat in a way the pagans weren't."

What fascinated Eugene TeSelle about the Donatist issue was that love was more important than the truth. "It was precisely for the sake of the love and peace of the church that Augustine wanted to coerce the Donatists back in. So love became a principle of intolerance, even more than the truth."

"But," asked Neuhaus, "if the same love is to be extended to all people, including the pagans, why would Augustine use coercion with the Donatists and not with the pagans?"

"Because they're the ones who appear to be inside, they're sealed with the seal of baptism," said TeSelle.

The dynamic at play in Augustine's attitude toward the the Donatists reminded Neuhaus of the sociological theory of propinquity and hostility, and how it is that often one opposes most vehemently those to whom one bears closest theological resemblance.

III. AUGUSTINE ON SEXUALITY

If the first day's conversation dealt with general themes in Augustine's thought, the second day focused on specific topics. The first of these was Father Robert O'Connell's presentation on sexuality. O'Connell joked that his contribution came "from my immense distance from this subject experientially."

Dualism, Ancient and Modern

A consensus quickly emerged that the standard charge of a radical dichotomy between body and soul in Augustine's thought is simply unfounded. "Maybe there are traces of that in his very earliest works," said O'Connell, "but he comes out of it very swiftly."

With that in mind, Georgetown University's James Schall questioned O'Connell: "Whenever I ask my Augustine students the question, 'Is man by nature evil?,' they almost invariably say: 'Yes, Augustine held that man is by nature evil.' I then say to them, 'Look, Augustine was an orthodox Christian, and he couldn't possibly hold that position!' The orthodox doctrine would be this: No, human nature would remain the same, but yes, it has a tendency to evil. How would you look on Augustine's understanding of original sin in this context?"

O'Connell did not disguise his delight at Schall's question. Said the Fordham professor: "At this point I'm supposed to say, 'I'm so glad you asked that question!' Most of you know the drum I've been beating over the last thirty years. My theory is that Augustine thought of us as fallen souls. It's my contention that Augustine clearly held that our souls once existed in some contemplative bliss, like the angels, and we committed some sin that turned us away from that contemplative life into the life of time and action. That was Origen's theory, and it was alive and well until at least about 415. That means that even before we were conceived we were sinful, and we came into life with that dynamic of sin already underway. That dynamic of sin begins to spell itself out specifically in a triad of sins: pride, curiosity, and eventually concupiscence. But these are simply workings out of the dynamic of sin with which we entered life."

And so O'Connell forged this answer for Schall's students: "It's something like this: Are we by nature evil? No, but by our own commission, and even before we are conceived, we are sinners, and that sin is working itself out even now. That's why on certain things that we understand as quite conventional human phenomena, like linguistic communication, Augustine is trying to get us to sense that something is damnably strange.

You're boxed in, and I'm boxed in, and I'm trying to get what's inside my box into yours, and I've got to use all these symbolic roundabout ways of doing it. Isn't that strange?"

Robert Wilken proposed a shorter answer to Schall's question: "The answer is that Augustine is not orthodox."

"He is not orthodox by our standards of orthodoxy," replied O'Connell. "Because the church condemned Origen's theory."

This left Gil Meilaender confused about how O'Connell would agree so quickly that the charge of Augustine's dualism is false. Meilaender wondered if some form of dualism was much deeper in Augustine than in O'Connell's reading of Augustine.

"There's an attenuated dualism," said O'Connell. "Augustine's theory of the fall comes to mean far more a theory of our having fallen from the altitude of contemplation into the relentless chase of temporal action."

"So the dualism is more a matter of time versus eternity," summarized Neuhaus.

"Time versus eternity is another way of precisely situating that dualism," agreed O'Connell. "But the fall is not a fall on account of a desire for the body. It doesn't have to be that at all. Is the result of the fall a kind of permanent severed relationship between the soul and body? Augustine would say, 'I thought that way once, but I realized that was a facile way of thinking of it, and maybe a residue of Manichaeism.' The real crunch comes between time and eternity, between contemplation and action. It's a different sort of dualism, as I see it now."

"But," asked Meilaender, "wouldn't you still want to get out of the body?"

"Perhaps," thought O'Connell. "But Augustine's Neoplatonic dualism was a lot friendlier to the body than a Manichaean dualism."

William Babcock suggested that it was unreasonable to expect to rescue Augustine completely from a sense of dualism. Babcock commented: "Despite the fact that everyone does it, it really isn't helpful to speak of any position from this period or earlier in the history of Christianity as dualistic, as if there was some non-dualistic option. You can't find any. The critical question is, In what respect is he a dualist? How exactly is the dualistic position held?"

O'Connell thought that Augustine did see one non-dualistic option: "He calls it materialism."

"But I really don't think that there was a live non-dualistic option that anyone was in fact willing to hold," said Babcock.

Eugene Teselle wanted to demythologize the discussion about dualism: "Dualisms come from general characteristics of human experience. Here our mind is inside a box, or our mind has all sorts of ideas but we're limited by our bodies, or we want to do one thing and our sexual member does something else. There are all sorts of dualisms in our experience." TeSelle then invoked Greg Jones's distinction concerning ends: "The inclusive end is the better way to describe these dualisms, where you can put things in a larger context. With the other option, dominant ends, it becomes a zero-sum game."

"One should opt for a more existential interpretation," TeSelle suggested, "in which one acknowledges that human life intrinsically has all these problems and conflicts. In a sense, the denial of that may be a problem."

O'Connell agreed: " 'What's the problem?' is my answer. We're the ones who make it a problem if we conceive that human life should really run along on some angelic lines, with perfect transparence between one another, absolute and instantaneous communication, and no difficulty getting up in the morning. But that's not the human condition, buddy."

"It's also a problem for someone like Feuerbach," said TeSelle. "For him, human nature has boundless possibilities which cannot be adequately expressed in action at any particular time. There are all sorts of different ways of putting it, but that is the human dilemma, isn't it?"

"Manichaeism is alive and well!" exclaimed O'Connell. "No one ever had to invent dualism. We're natural dualists in the way we resent our human condition."

But Karen Torjesen took exception to the notion that the dualistic structure of the world came out of our experience. She argued that dualism is, in fact, invented. "Dualism is more of a cultural construct than a biological experience. The Semitic notion of the self is not dualistic, it's a primitive unity. The dualism we're talking about is a conceptual system that has its origins in classical Greece. What conditions led to that? I believe the answer lies in looking at the way the body and sexuality are defined by the social constructs of classical Athens. In classical Athens you have a slaveholding, patriarchal society, in which authority is exercised through violence against the body. So the body is the symbol for the means of exercising social dominance. Therefore it also becomes a symbol for weakness."

Neuhaus asked if she was suggesting that there was available to Augustine a non-dualistic option. No, thought Torjesen, because by his time all such options had been eliminated.

Augustine, Sexuality, and Creation: Coming into Port?

Neuhaus turned the conversation to sexuality: "We have to relate dualism to the question of Augustine's understanding of the well-ordered life. Among the interesting things in O'Connell's paper is that he denies the idea of any constructive or redemptive role for sexuality. In Augustine's thought, sexuality is almost always the threat to be contained or controlled. If that's true, it's very much at the heart of the general condemnation of Augustine, and his influence, in some quarters of the Christian tradition." Neuhaus then asked whether that conventional wisdom about Augustine was justified.

Graham Walker contended that it was precisely in his treatment of sexuality that Augustine arrived at a non-dualistic view of the body-soul problem. "When he gets to sexuality, Augustine has, in a sense, brought his ship into home port. That is, he has finally reached a fundamentally non-dualistic view of sexuality, and of body and soul. It seems to me that the pole star by which he's navigating his ship into this home port is the idea of creation. His mature view, once he gets to port, seems to be that all these poignantly crosscutting tensions of human experience are not the result of our embodied natures but are the result of the vitiation of our embodied natures.

"And so original sin and all of its dynamics — including the obstreperousness of sexuality, all that poignantly crosscutting stuff — have to do with a deficiency. It is an overlay on top of what is an intrinsically good, embodied human nature.

"Fallenness is an inescapable reality, but it's a subsidiary reality and not the primary reality. Thus it is not finally dualistic. It is realistic, but not dualistic."

But O'Connell countered that, according to Augustine, "the primary thing that hits you when you inspect human experience is that something is profoundly wrong."

"Yes," conceded Walker, "profoundly wrong, but that wrongness is not intrinsic to human nature."

O'Connell remained unpersuaded. "Well, you can have these fine notions of what the Edenic condition was before sin. These are all very nice. But look at our situation. That's what we've got to deal with."

Greg Jones stepped in to mediate this exchange. "Graham wants to say that, at an ontological level, Augustine is not dualistic. But experientially, when he looks at humans as we are in this world, he sees that it's dualistic."

Others wondered if Walker was trying to trim Augustine to fit modern patterns of orthodoxy. The discussion then centered on the appropriation of the past for the present.

"As a historian, I would have to object strongly to Walker's reading of Augustine," said Paula Fredriksen. "Graham is basically saying that what coheres with a twentieth-century reading is what is ontologically prior in Augustine's formulation, and what is irreducibly fifth century is really an aside in his argument. If we're going to have dualism mean anything, that's the world Augustine inhabits. He goes beyond his previous statements remarkably, and that's because of his biblical rootedness. But I wouldn't want to say that it's all really one thing and it's cheese, and the fallenness is cheeselessness, like the holes in Swiss cheese."

But Fredriksen did not convince Neuhaus. "Given our twentieth-century vocabulary, isn't it accurate for us to say in our time that one can properly understand Augustine as ontologically saying that the 'really real' is good?"

"We can use Augustine if we choose to construct a modern theology and cite him," said Fredriksen. "And if we want to make the case that we are not dualists. And we're not dualists in the way that late antiquity was. That is just a way of saying we live in a different period. But I don't think we can say that's what Augustine was doing."

"Is it really so implausible that Augustine could have had a new idea?" asked Walker. "He could have been profoundly non-dualistic even though it didn't fit in its historical *zeitgeist*."

Fredriksen was prepared to grant that Augustine did have a good idea. But, she insisted, that didn't make it unique and different from his time.

As the charges of anachronism and historicism were being exchanged, Gil Meilaender tried formulating the question in different way. "What if you gave the *City of God* to a student, and you said, 'Read it, there's a lot of truth to be found here.' Is that an objectionable formulation?"

Neuhaus went further. "If you handed someone the mature Augustine, and if he or she drew from it something like what Graham drew from it, and said, 'Yes, that's a good way to understand human nature,' is that an abuse of Augustine?"

William Babcock responded to Neuhaus with a logical point, arguing that one could respond positively to Meilaender but negatively to Walker. "You can agree with any claim that says the book will teach you something that is true, and yet disagree with what it is that the book actually teaches you. Augustine comes up with a sinless, pre-fall sexuality. However, what Augustine says about post-fall sexuality, one might not like."

Elizabeth Clarke agreed: "If you mentioned to a modern student a specific point about Augustine's view of sexuality, namely that it is venially sinful for married couples to engage in sexual intercourse without first and foremost thinking about their procreation of a child, what do you suppose a modern student would say?"

No one thought that Clarke's student would be positively impressed with Augustine's teaching. Still, Meilander stuck to his guns: "Granted, Augustine may have had a distorted notion of the person. But Augustine can still have profound insight into some truth about human nature, and I don't think that that claim can be overturned by pointing to one historically idiosyncratic feature."

Fredriksen conceded that someone could read Augustine as a contemporary from whom one might learn something about sexuality. "But that only gives you personal information about me and how I construct personhood today. That is not to say that I would want to look at Augustine's theology and analyze it in terms of what turns out to be congenial to me."

Rabbi David Novak ventured that this discussion among Christians could benefit from the perspective of an outsider. Said Novak: "There's a fundamental problem that has to be brought out in the open. The problem that you have with Augustine is the problem that I have with Maimonides. Are we talking about what Maimonides meant or about the truth of what Maimonides said? Now if we're talking about what he meant, then we should incorporate all the linguistic, historical skills that we have at our disposal, and say what he meant in the proper context. If we're asking whether what he's saying is true, then we are asking what Maimonides said is true about Judaism as we experience it here and now.

"Similarly, if you're asking the question, Is Augustine true?, then you can sort out certain elements and indicate there are things that he said that are still true about the truth that you call Christianity. That has to be your focus. This is not only a conference of Augustine scholars. This is also a group primarily of Christians, a group that regards Christianity, in some way or another, as true. The question is, What does Augustine of Hippo have to say that sheds light upon that truth which you affirm? What does Augustine say about sexuality for Christians today?

"That's the hermeneutical problem that you have. Are you looking for the meaning only? Or are you looking for the truth? Obviously truth presupposes meaning. But meaning doesn't always presuppose truth. The focus of our discussion has wavered between the experts who are talking about the meaning of Augustine and the broader theological interests of the truth. But the truth is a Christian truth, the truth of a specific community. The question is, At this stage of your 'story,' to use Stanley Hauerwas's term, how much does Augustine shed light on the truth that you affirm?"

Wilken contended that Novak was being unfair to the historians in implying that they lacked theological interests. "It is possible to be a historian and also to take responsibility for one's tradition," he insisted. "My point is that there were other Christians who dealt differently with these issues than Augustine did. Augustine is part of a developing tradition. He has come down on certain sides. And there are other people who came down on other sides. If one is interested in Augustine's influence on the Christian tradition, then it is of great importance to know what he actually said, its good and bad sides, and how he influenced the later tradition.

"But if our goal is not to rehabilitate Augustine," Wilken continued, "but to think Christianly about the issue of sexuality, then why do we have to find the one Augustinian formula that we can now live with? Why not simply admit that, at least in some areas, Augustine led us astray? There are other people who can perhaps aid us in talking Christianly about sexuality. It isn't as though everything has to come from Augustine. If we were talking about a church dogma, say the Nicene dogma, then I think we would have a different attitude. But we are talking about a Christian thinker, not the dogmatic voice."

Neuhaus then rose to defend Walker: "So we don't have to say that Augustine was right on all these things. But is anyone saying that? Graham's point is that when Augustine came to port, when he was finally settled, here is what he was saying, in our twentieth-century terms. Then Graham turns the question to the historians. He asks if it is fair to say that this is a reasonable appropriation of the mature Augustine in our time. That is not saying that we're obligated to find that Augustine was right."

A missing aspect to this discussion on sexuality, according to Ernest Fortin, was the nature of the fall. "There is a moral dimension to the fall," Fortin asserted, "and maybe a metaphysical dimension to it as well. I don't think there's a metaphysical dualism, but there is a moral dualism of sorts. The difficulty with the fall is explaining why it happened in the first instance. How can bad fruit come from a good tree?" Fortin was curious if O'Connell had an answer to that.

O'Connell acknowledged that the fall was a most difficult thing to explain in Neoplatonism. "How are you going to understand that a being like our soul, in that absolutely ecstatic unity that comes with the mystical rapture of being, would desert its own beatitude? Augustine and Plotinus both strain heroically to explain that. Distraction and satiation are two explanations. Plotinus has as many explanations of it as he has moods, and that rubs off on Augustine too.

"But I think Ernie will admit that instead of it being merely a moral fall, it is an attempt on the part of Neoplatonists and Augustine to make the moral a metaphysical rhyme. If we are lower in the metaphysical order, it is because we have become lower in the moral order. That was Augustine's attempt all the way through. I don't think he ever wanted to talk of moral declension or moral deterioration apart from a necessary association with metaphysical deterioration."

Some participants felt that the conversation hadn't resolved the question of the mature Augustine. William Babcock brought up Augustine's view of the instrumentality of sexuality. "Sexuality is integral to the person, as human beings are created male and female. But sexuality is purely instrumental for the begetting of children. The interpersonal relationship of husband and wife cannot be expressed by sexuality because it will be *cupiditas.* That's the real Augustinian view of marriage, isn't it?"

O'Connell followed: "I remember when Augustine asked why God gave man a woman, and the obvious answer was procreation. One of his clinching arguments was that if God had given Adam somebody for the delights of companionship, he would obviously have given him another man!

"Is sexuality integral to the person? It chills me to read *De Trinitate* in that connection. Augustine asks what it means when we say that man is created in the image of God. He shears away sense, faith, action, and he gets to the point where man is contemplative mind. And that is the most central thing you say about man. What is integral to man is only what pertains to him as contemplative mind. That's the gasoline that fuels Augustine's view of sexuality."

"Sexuality is both integral and incidental," said Babcock. "We were created in the body. The body is integral to the way human beings are created. But sexuality is incidental. It's only a small part of the total human task."

That's a proper dualism, TeSelle added, a proper subordination of the body, and especially sexuality, to the real human task.

"Monica Today"

At this point Jean Elshtain wondered how much of the discussion of Augustine and the body was prejudiced by contemporary assumptions about sexuality. She raised her concern by way of what she called a "Monica Today" question. "I thought that Bob O'Connell's paper was pretty rough on Augustine's mother at some points. He refers to Monica as a puritanically righteous wife, and he indicates that she had a censorious view of sexuality. As I read that I thought, 'here we go again, with Monica taking her lumps!'

"But then it struck me that interesting questions presented themselves about the possible constructions of female sexuality in late antiquity. O'Connell presupposes some set of standards as to what would count as puritanically righteous and censorious." Elshtain alluded to Karen Torjesen's earlier comment on constructions of embodiment in late antiquity. "We privilege the sexual, we weight it enormously in our story of the self. In this post-Freudian era, it's almost inevitable that we would locate sexuality as essential. It seems to me that O'Connell is sneaking some of that privileging of sexuality into his characterizations.

"There were other kinds of concerns about embodiment that would have preoccupied our foremothers and forefathers that are not practical issues with us. Consider the enormous fragility of the body, with its range of illnesses and possibility of starvation, and compare that to what we can take for granted today. The body was fragile in all kinds of ways that it isn't for us, because these other problems of our mortal bodies have gone into relative abeyance. That has perhaps created the space for us then to become preoccupied with the sexual features of embodiment."

O'Connell's defense was a reminder that it is Augustine who writes the *Confessions*. Thus it is Augustine's explanation, and Augustine chooses to write the scenario from Patricius's point of view, not Monica's.

The remarks that several had made about Augustine's negative influence on sexuality prompted Robert Markus to comment: "I think that there is an ambivalence about the notion of legacy itself, which ought to be highlighted. I very much agree with many here that, on the whole, Augustine's influence on the development of Western Christian thought on sexuality has been wholly baleful. But I think it is important to realize what one means when one is saying that. It is clear that Augustine is holding a far more positive view about the matter than almost anyone else. Just think: Had he not engaged in this controversy, we might still be talking like Jerome, or like Ambrose, or like the Cappadocians. I think that at least one achievement that one has to credit Augustine with is that it will never be possible to speak about human sexuality in the way that Jerome spoke about it. I think that is an important reverse side to this question."

O'Connell concluded with some general comments about Augustine's relationship with his contemporaries. In response to the concerns of Robert Wilken, O'Connell was willing to recognize the "bullying characteristics" in Augustine's polemics. But those characteristics must be understood, he explained, in terms of Augustine's era. "In those days the art of ecclesiastical billingsgate was quite advanced. You could call somebody a heretic in seven different ways!"

How aware should Augustine have been to alternative views of sexuality? O'Connell was prepared to grant Augustine the benefit of the doubt. "Augustine was in Africa, and ideas traveled very slowly in those days. I wouldn't be so sure that he was nearly so acquainted with adversarial forms of thought as we would hope."

O'Connell concluded on a speculative note. He compared Augustine to Teilhard de Chardin, wishing that each had an adversary his equal. If Augustine had had an orthodox and intelligent theological adversary to engage him on the matter of human sexuality, the history of the West might have been vastly different.

IV. AUGUSTINE ON JUSTICE

In turning its attention to Eugene TeSelle's paper, the conversation shifted to that modern obsession, politics. Presenter Eugene TeSelle pointed out that Augustine had been canonized in the strand of political thought called realism, and Jean Elshtain wanted to explore that point.

Augustine vs. the Realists

"I think Gene quite rightly pointed out that this is a very partial reading of Augustine," Elshtain said. "There are so many dramatic ways in which Augustine differs from the 'realpolitikers' that we ought to dislodge him from their clutches." She went on to describe the ways of dislodging him. "For Augustine the ideal of a commonwealth is defined by the sharing of objects of love, and by the ordering and evaluating of those particular loves. Augustine endorses a profoundly social understanding of human beings and their relations to others, in contrast to the asociality of a Hobbes. Augustine argues in behalf of a naturalistic morality shared by the whole human race, a sense of shame, a sense of limits. The metaphor of the social contract is not one that he deploys. It's not one that would have been known to him particularly, certainly not one that he would endorse. And he also provides, in contrast to the realists, a way to evaluate established orders as in fact profoundly disordered. He can look at an order imposed by a coercive power like Rome and say, 'They call this peace, but this is a profoundly disordered polity.' So in those ways he really doesn't belong in the modern realist camp. Indeed, you can use Augustine to argue against many of realism's presuppositions, even though he also insists, with it, on the recognition of pervasive conflict in human affairs, the tensions, the imperfectness, and the incompleteness of this world. That is, he's strongly anti-utopian."

"But," Elshtain went on to ask, "if we are to pry him loose from the realist construction of reality, where then do we relocate him? Is he within another tradition of thought, or is he *sui generis*?"

She answered her own question: "The one great twentieth-century philosopher who turned to Augustine repeatedly was Hannah Arendt. What she found in Augustine that figures in all of her work is the power of his argument against the cyclical theory of history. He creates space for new beginnings that the cyclical theory denies. He also has the profound sense of living in fallen times. Arendt calls them dark times. It's something like an updated version of the fall, of having fallen into time, and what that means for our political possibilities and our political hopes. Also much of her politics is about keeping the worst from happening; she knows that there are all kinds of terrible possibilities in the world of human affairs. Arendt is profoundly critical of the sacralization of the state, and she sees that as an inappropriate idolization and sacralization of politics."

TeSelle wanted to allow for a couple of possible Augustinian positions on politics. "One is basically a sense of duty. That leads to the coercion of the Donatists. It's also often characteristic of his just-war thinking: a deductive, deontological reasoning which says that if the rule tells you to do it, you go and do it.

"Another possibility is *Realpolitik*. You may have to despair; but it doesn't matter what kind of regime human beings fated to death live under. You may have to do what you must and say your prayers.

"But finally you've got to come out with a sense of the relative and transient. That which is changeable, no matter how much you may achieve, intrinsically poses a threat. But you've got to live within those terms. You've got to set finite goals for yourself. That's precisely the problem in politics — people don't like finite goals for themselves."

"And so," Neuhaus asked, "would you like to see Augustine liberated from what Jean describes as the realist tradition?"

"Yes," TeSelle said.

"What's intriguing and of continuing importance about Augustine," Elshtain added, "is that you can bring him to bear as a critic of political realism as it exists in our own time. But he doesn't lapse into an overly optimistic set of utopian construals. He can't be deployed for utopian purposes, because of his emphasis on the pervasiveness of conflict. It's more difficult for the realists to dismiss Augustine than it is for them to dismiss a whole range of other thinkers that they see as blithely utopian about the political possibility. Augustine is a tougher case for them."

TeSelle suspected that "Reinhold Niebuhr, at his best, would resemble Augustine here, because Niebuhr represents persistence without cynicism. I think when Niebuhr was an ideologist on the Cold War, I could explain out of Augustine what he did wrong there."

"Augustine might have seen that as an application of a Manichaean absolutism, or sliding in that direction, in temporal affairs," said Elshtain.

Graham Walker was less willing to separate Augustine from realism. "Augustine sort of fits with the social-contract people, like Machiavelli, Hobbes, and yet he doesn't. One clue seems to be available in history: where was it in fact that these radically modern, social-contract theories took hold? It was precisely in those cultures whose popular mind-set was mostly formed by an Augustinian version of Christianity. That is, mostly Protestant cultures. It was those people who swallowed Hobbesian and Lockean social-contract theory, but with a grain of salt. Even though the intellectuals were rabidly modern, still the common folk in those polities, including our own at its founding, could buy it, except that they held it at arm's length, because they were Augustinian in their theology. They had the sense that there was God, there was goodness, and yet in this world there's this fallen condition, and this social-contract thing works fairly well." So Walker wanted to locate Augustine in what he termed the "ameliorative social reform of believing Protestants." And he agreed that Niebuhr in his best days would fit that picture.

"Niebuhr would not be in the Hobbesian tradition at all?" asked Neuhaus.

"Only at arm's length, and with a grain of salt," said Walker.

The Best Regime

The question of where to locate Augustine prompted Ernest Fortin to confess a sense of "something missing" in Augustine as a political thinker. "To put it in simple terms," Fortin began, "there is no discussion of the best regime. How can you improve your society? What are the different possibilities? There is a great interest in Augustine in society and its problems. But when you ask if someone is a political thinker, you generally look for an interest in the nitty-gritty. This is a practical science, after all.

"Augustine had a certain indifference with regard to these things. 'What difference does it make under which regime you live? You're going to end up dead anyway,' Augustine seems to say. Show me Augustine's discussion of the best regime," Fortin challenged the group.

"I think there is a theological answer, and it relates to your question of where to put him," said Gil Meilaender. "I don't think you put him in any of those great traditions. In *Christ and Culture*, H. Richard Niebuhr puts Augustine — a little uncertainly, because of the realist dimension — in the transformist category. What the transformist can do is find intimations of the truth in a lot of different political theorists, but can't belong to any of them. And similarly, we couldn't possibly construct the best regime because, if we had one, we'd have to transform it again right away. That dynamic movement would have to keep on going as long as human history goes on."

The problem of the best regime lay at the heart of the *City of God*, according to Robert Markus. The only good regime, let alone the best regime, is one which cannot be established by human agency. "So what does Augustine settle for?" Markus asked. "Rather than describing any one of a number of alternative possible utopias, he talks about a state in which you do the best that you can in purely pragmatic terms. This is the point of the *City of God*. It is to formulate a concept of the *res publica* to which the Christian and the pagan alike will be able to give loyalty. That is the fundamental point, once you get all the polemics out of the way: how to speak of an ideologically neutral community."

"Is that true?" asked TeSelle. "Let me put forward an alternative. The *City of God* is apologetic. Despite the fall of Rome, Augustine contends, Christianity is still viable. After looking at the pagan definitions of the true republic you find that the only true republic is in heaven, and we've got an inferior imitation of it on earth. The first purpose is argumentative, apologetic, to refute the pagan objections; only then, as an afterthought, there's the common ground."

The Least Common Denominator

Markus used the question of common ground as an opportunity to raise the problem of the least common denominator. "I've never seen the solution to this. Augustine defines community in terms of what its members have in common. It seems to follow necessarily that the more comprehensive the community the lower the object to which it can owe common allegiance. Augustine describes communities where the fundamental loyalties are all too diverse. All that you have agreement on are those basic components of the earthly things. Of course you would like to raise their sights and to have a qualitatively higher level of common commitment. But how do you raise their sights?"

"Yes, this is a problem," agreed TeSelle, and he suggested that Augustine recognized the consequences. "He would have liked to have a world of small realms. What we've got now is an empire which is breaking down of its own weight, and people are isolated individuals.

"Let's turn to another side of it," TeSelle continued. "There are various values that can hold a society together. I was suggesting, as a minimum, that we're all in the same boat. This may mean different things in different periods of human history: such as fending off the barbarians or worrying about nuclear winter. But that is at least a minimum basis of human community."

Markus agreed, but he still wanted to move from that minimum to Augustine's concerns for a higher level of common commitment. He added: "What kind of criteria do you appeal to in order to raise your sights?"

TeSelle guessed that perhaps the society of the least common denominator is the most just form of society. "Maybe talking precisely about those very basic things is what we mean by a just society. Let the religious things be religious, and not get them mixed in together."

Jean Elshtain suggested that the answer to Markus's question was a "willed redirection" of the objects of love. Elshtain noted: "Augustine could imagine a situation, with conflict and ongoing temptation, where a true commonweal had been approximated through redirection. This meant transformation in human willing, transformation in the objects that are loved in common. Rather than a dispersion of the self into all these many points of lustful fixation, Augustine could imagine something like a gathering in of the self, and then a redirection."

But, responded Markus, "the problem is far more serious because it's the question of the redirection of a group."

William Babcock sympathized with Markus's dilemma, and he described the problem more pointedly: "I want to see if we couldn't understand these societies bound together by common love, at least in the nonheavenly case, as being a little more vociferous than TeSelle suggested they are, more in danger of splintering apart. The reason is that *cupiditas*; the love that creates the earthly city is a collective noun. There are *cupiditates*; there are lots of them. That's why this earthly community is held together not by common love but by a temporal law. Temporal law adjudicates the ways in which people can and cannot pursue their various *cupiditates* to make sure that they don't do harm to each other."

Babcock returned to Elshtain's comment about the transformation of willing: "By the time Augustine writes the *City of God*, he knows very well how wills are changed. They are changed by God, they are not changed by others. This insight produces some interesting consequences for Augustine. Why should we rebuke people? What's the point of rebuking someone if we know very well that the rebuke isn't going to take unless God changes the will? Well, Augustine's answer is that you've got to do it. If it takes, it shows that God wanted to use your rebuke. If it doesn't, it still isn't a complete waste of time, because the person deserves to be rebuked anyway. You can rebuke, and the outcome is not determined by human factors, it is only determined by God."

So, can you attempt to ameliorate society? "Yes," thought Babcock, "because you have an obligation to do that. But if it is not going to work, it is not necessarily your fault."

Elshtain confessed that this left her with a conundrum. "On the one hand," she said, "the transformation of willing is required in order to reform institutions. On the other hand, Augustine is clear about the nature of the institutions and social relations in which we find ourselves. You've got a tension, a tug and pull. That's not unique to him; it's also stated very powerfully by Rousseau in the social contract. The kinds of virtues that ought to be present in order to create the just republic are the kind of virtues that flow from being a citizen in the just republic. And Augustine just leaves it at that paradox."

Augustine Today

Neuhaus picked up on the question about the fostering of the coherence of wills and the comment on the purpose of the *City of God*, and he tied them together to direct the group into a summary discussion on the appropriation of Augustine for today. Said Neuhaus: "It seems to me that those two questions are very closely related, and they are pertinent to the question of Augustine today. If there is any question that agitates our pluralistic society, it is how you find that commonality that real, Bible-believing, conservative, Jesus-is-going-to-come-again Christians can take seriously, with authentic Christian seriousness. The question of the common definition of the *res publica* is the whole question of mediating language. Mediating language is the language that mediates from a particular belief system, Christianity, and engages in a genuinely public discourse with people who do not necessarily subscribe to that system. If that's what Augustine was doing, it suggests that Augustine was terribly important to what clearly needs to be done in our society. It's something like an exercise in public philosophy, a religiously grounded and informed public philosophy.

"And if Augustine's transformative direction discovers the ways in which differently ordered wills might be brought into coherence with one another for the right ordering of the civil realm, then that is a strongly suggestive argument that the *City of God* is terrifically pertinent to the most urgent questions in dispute about public life today."

William Babcock wasn't sure if he agreed with Markus on the purpose of the *City of God*. But, he continued, "it is important to acknowledge, for whatever political or sociological use one is going to make of the *City of God*, that Augustine knows where the convergence of wills takes place. It takes place at only one point, earthly peace, and even there the two cities converge for different reasons. The earthly city wants earthly peace so that it can enjoy the things that it wants to enjoy. And the heavenly city wants earthly peace so that it can enjoy what it wants to enjoy, which incidentally is what all ought to enjoy but only some do."

"But that low level of convergence is not to speak against Augustine's argument, is it?" countered Neuhaus. "It's only to illuminate how our culture has inflated political expectations. One of the strengths of Augustine's argument is that it debunks and radically relativizes the imperiousness of the political as such, which makes it all the more politically potent, as a suggestive way of right ordering."

On the general question of appropriation, Robert Wilken asserted that, on balance, Augustine's influence has been for the good. But he raised the question of Eastern Christianity's neglect of Augustine: "Here is a thinker whom we hold so dear as Westerners. But there is a whole Christian tradition that has not even read him."

Meilaender wasn't ready to concede that the Eastern neglect of Augustine was necessarily a mark against him. It might be that Eastern Christianity could have found some political wisdom in the *City of God*, and he urged Wilken not to overlook that possibility.

Wilken continued to debate the question of theologically appropriating the past: "There has been a profound shift in the way in which we now must deal with this question, because Augustine is now studied by a whole range of scholars who are not committed to the Christian tradition. It's a question of faith and reason in the sense of whether the Christian reading of the Christian past is a reading which is reasonable to people who do not share Christian commitments. So it is of some importance, then, that one get the details correct and that one set them in historical context. It's not that one is trying to avoid the theological problems, but if we are to be reasonable, the way we describe this person has to be recognizable to all concerned." We have a new situation, Wilken insisted, and that new situation is that we can no longer read the past simply as a group of Christian scholars.

Greg Jones added another qualification to the question of appropriation. "There is a temptation," he noted, "to presume that Augustine speaks *ex cathedra,* or that he is in the canon of Scripture. To look to others is not necessarily to denigrate Augustine's relevance, but it is to say that there are other perspectives that in some ways may be more satisfying than Augustine."

Gil Meilaender challenged what he perceived to be a hidden assumption at work in this discussion. That assumption is that to appropriate Augustine, he must be found to be a blessing, not a bane, and that the Augustine we discover must be positive and affirmative about human history. Meilaender reminded everyone that this had been a stumbling block in the earlier discussion of sexuality. The working assumption there was that Augustine had influenced the aesthetic-mystical paradigm in Western Christendom. But Meilaender wondered if, in Augustine's politics, a similar paradigm wasn't at work: "In political matters, Augustine is willing to say on a lot of occasions that it really doesn't matter. In a sense, only the City of God ultimately matters." And maybe, Meilaender went on to suggest, this is precisely what we need to appropriate from him. "Maybe what our world needs is to learn again that none of these earthly things satisfy the human heart. That may be the essential Augustine. Rather than assuming that we have to find something that's a little more positive than that, we should consider that to be a message that carries its own power and force."

Meilander struck a note with James Schall. Said Schall: "As I look over the history of my own education, it seems to me that the first thing I ever heard about Augustine was that Augustine was the source of all heresies in the church! My education was vaguely anti-Augustinian in the beginning, but as I get older, I get more and more Augustinian. As Gil was saying, less and less do I see the City of God as an earthly project. I've been very critical for the last fifteen to twenty years about the tendency in religion and in political philosophy toward utopianism. For me, Augustine has always been a cure for that."

Ernest Fortin suggested that Schall's education was not an exception, as Augustine suffers from a checkered legacy. But he said that Augustine has managed to be rehabilitated because some features of our cultural moment have led to an Augustinian reappropriation. Fortin continued: "I do think that there's more interest in authors of antiquity today than there has been for a long time. At the beginning of this century, nobody went back to them. Now all of a sudden the new interest in these authors has been created. There's an idea abroad that maybe they were wrong on some points, maybe they didn't know everything, but they *might* have the right approach. Their way of looking at the world in general may be more wholesome than ours. They didn't live in the kind of fractured or fragmented universe that we seem to be a part of. People are now asking, What have they got that we lack? There's a sense of something missing; we know that we don't have everything we should have and could have."

It was left to Gene TeSelle to sum up this discussion. "I was especially struck by Markus's comment about Augustine's desacralization. Christianity may have created desacralization. It took a long time, but it finally destroyed the temples, and it said that the public square is to be naked except for the Christian Church, which will be the one Christian Church. If desacralization of public life is a benefit, then is this the achievement of Christianity alone? Can it perhaps be done by natural reason? I would want to be on Markus's side on this point, and yes, in principle I think it can be done by simply looking at human life through the eyes of reason. In large part, that is what Augustine is doing in Book XIX of the *City of God*.

"What about religious pluralism in our own day? I think we are unwise to celebrate the patristic period for its defiance of Rome and the decline of tolerant religious pluralism of the ancient world. In our own world, we must engage in dialogue, not only with the great world religions, but with all religions, indigenous, new, and so forth. How do we cope with that? That is the new question, for which Augustine does not prepare us at all. He still insists on the one way of salvation and that has to be worked out in all of life — ecclesiastically, politically, and so on."

Neuhaus questioned why believing in one way of salvation prevented Augustine from engaging in respectful dialogue.

"At least it meant that he certainly didn't engage in respectful dialogue with the pagans or the philosophers or the Jews," reported TeSelle. "You could perhaps find the Augustinian principles for dialogue, but that was not his historical moment. He bought into the Theodosian solution of coerced belief. That's one of those marvelous historical problems. That's one of the reasons for his legacy being ambiguous."

Fredriksen asked if TeSelle was suggesting that what Augustine wrote in his own circumstances is a life-giving legacy to us. Can we find that in Augustine, given the fact that we don't have the option of recourse to the secular arm to impose religious uniformity?

TeSelle smiled. "That's the silver-lining side of it, isn't it? Augustine helped us to secularize. Secularization *can* mean religious pluralism, although it didn't in his historical moment."

On TeSelle's "silver lining" the conference drew to a close. While there was no final consensus about what constituted Augustine's legacy, everyone seemed to leave the conference with a greater conviction of the magnitude of that legacy. There was clearly a sense that, in Augustine of Hippo, all were engaged with a great and passionate mind that loved God, and the City of God, above all.

Participants

William S. Babcock
Perkins School of Theology
Southern Methodist
 University

Elizabeth A. Clark
Department of Religion
Duke University

Jean Bethke Elshtain
Department of Political
 Science
Vanderbilt University

Ernest L. Fortin
Department of Theology
Boston College

Paula Fredriksen
Department of Religious
 Studies
University of Pittsburgh

Paul R. Hinlicky
Lutheran Forum

L. Gregory Jones
Department of Theology
Loyola College in Maryland

Robert Markus
Early Christian Studies
 Program
The Catholic University of
 America

Joanne McWilliam
Faculty of Divinity
Trinity College
Toronto

Gilbert Meilaender
Department of Religion
Oberlin College

John R. Muether
Reformed Theological
 Seminary

Richard John Neuhaus
New York City

David Novak
Department of Religious
 Studies
University of Virginia

Robert J. O'Connell, S.J.
Department of Philosophy
Fordham University

157

James V. Schall, S.J.
Jesuit Community
Georgetown University

Paul T. Stallsworth
Creswell, NC

Walter Sundberg
Luther Northwestern
    Theological Seminary

Eugene TeSelle
The Divinity School
Vanderbilt University

Karen Jo Torjesen
Department of Religion
The Claremont Graduate
    School

Graham Walker
Department of Political
    Science
University of Pennsylvania

Robert Wilken
Department of Religious
    Studies
University of Virginia